Education for Critical Consciousness

Education for Critical Consciousness

PAULO FREIRE

CONTINUUM • New York

FOR CAROLINA

1992

The Continuum Publishing Company
370 Lexington Avenue, New York, N.Y. 10017

Original editions:
Educação como prática da Liberdade
Editoria Paz e Terra, Rio de Janeiro, 1969
Extensión y Comunicación
Institute for Agricultural Reform, Santiago (Chile), 1969

The English-language edition of *Education for Critical Consciousness* was prepared in association with the center for the Study of Development and Social Change, Cambridge, Massachusetts.

Printed in the United States of America

Library of Congress Catalog Card Number: 72-12830
ISBN: 0-8264-0007-8

Contents

Introduction

To think dialectically is to decree the obsolescence of cherished concepts which explain even one's recent past. One of the marks of a true dialectician, however, is the ability to "move beyond" the past without repudiating it in the name of new levels of critical consciousness presently enjoyed. No contemporary writer more persistently explores the many dimensions of critical consciousness than Paulo Freire, a multi-cultural educator with the whole world as his classroom notwithstanding the totally Brazilian flavor of his emotions, his language, and his universe of thought. Freire never tires of looking for new forms of critical consciousness and unearthing new links between oppression in a variety of settings and the liberating effects of "conscientização." The unifying thread in his work is critical consciousness as the motor of cultural emancipation.

The publication in English at this time of two essays written by Freire in 1965 and 1968, respectively, aims at recapturing for U.S. readers what Paulo Freire calls the *"naïveté* of his thought" at the time of writing. Faithful to the historicity of human experience, Freire refuses to disown, even while transcending, his past writings and actions. If such fidelity troubles readers who would make of "conscientização" or of Freire himself a myth or an object of consumption, so be it! Freire is the first to rejoice in thus gaining a new weapon against mystification.

"Education as the Practice of Freedom" grows out of Paulo Freire's creative efforts in adult literacy throughout Brazil prior to the military coup of April 1, 1964, which eventually resulted in his exile. Were the piece to be written today, I feel certain that its title would become "Education as the Praxis of Liberation." For although Freire's earlier work does view action as *praxis,* the precise symbiosis between reflective action and critical theorizing is the fruit of later works, especially *Cultural Action for Freedom* and

Pedagogy of the Oppressed. Similarly, Freire's notion of freedom has always been dynamic and rooted in the historical process by which the oppressed struggle unremittingly to "extroject" (the term is his) the slave consciousness which oppressors have "introjected" into the deepest recesses of their being. Yet in recent years Freire has grown ever more attentive to the special oppression masked by the forms of democratic "freedom" or civil "liberty." Accordingly, he now emphasizes liberation as being both a dynamic activity and the partial conquest of those engaged in dialogical education.

American readers of *Pedagogy of the Oppressed* will find in "Education as the Practice of Freedom" the basic components of Freire's literacy method. These elements are

- participant observation of educators "tuning in" to the vocabular universe of the people;
- their arduous search for generative words at two levels: syllabic richness and a high charge of experiential involvement;
- a first codification of these words into visual images which stimulate people "submerged" in the culture of silence to "emerge" as conscious makers of their own "culture";
- the decodification by a "culture circle" under the self-effacing stimulus of a coordinator who is no "teacher" in the conventional sense, but who has become an educator-educatee—in dialogue with educatee-educators too often treated by formal educators as passive recipients of knowledge;
- a creative new codification, this one explicitly critical and aimed at action, wherein those who were formerly illiterate now begin to reject their role as mere "objects" in nature and social history and undertake to become "subjects" of their own destiny.

They now perceive their own illiteracy as the cultural artifact of those who would oppress them. This is a first release from those written words which their oppressors had kept imprisoned in the magic tool-box of those present-day sorcerers, the stewards of the culture of silence. One spontaneously thinks here of Levi-Strauss as he discusses the special awe, almost religious in character, experienced by primitives in the presence of those who master the arts of writing. Education in the Freire mode is the practice of liberty because it frees the educator no less than the educatees from the twin thraldom of silence and monologue. Both partners are liberated as they begin to learn, the one to know self as a being of worth—notwithstanding the stigma of illiteracy, poverty, or technological ignorance— and the other as capable of dialogue in spite of the strait jacket imposed by the role of educator as one who knows.

Paulo Freire's central message is that one can know only to the extent that one "problematizes" the natural, cultural and historical reality in which s/he is immersed. Problematizing is the antithesis of the technocrat's "problem-solving" stance. In the latter approach, an expert takes some distance from reality, analyzes it into component parts, devises means for resolving difficulties in the most efficient way, and then dictates a strategy or policy. Such problem-solving, according to Freire, distorts the totality of human experience by reducing it to those dimensions which are amenable to treatment as mere difficulties to be solved. But to "problematize" in his sense is to associate an entire populace to the task of codifying total reality into symbols which can generate critical consciousness and empower them to alter their relations with nature and social forces. This reflective group exercise is rescued from narcissism or psychologism only if it thrusts all participants into dialogue with others whose historical "vocation" is to become transforming agents of their social reality. Only thus do people become subjects, instead of objects, of their own history.

Such language may appear unduly Promethean to those who fear ecological disaster or who seek to reinstate a Zen, Tao, or Sufi contemplative posture as a corrective to the over-active West. But Freire is no ethnocentric reductionist: he knows that action without critical reflection and even without gratuitous contemplation is disastrous activism. Conversely, he insists that theory or introspection in the absence of collective social action is escapist idealism or wishful thinking. In his view, genuine theory can only be derived from some *praxis* rooted in historical struggles. This is the reason why Freire cannot be the theorist of social revolution in the United States, although many of his hearers unconsciously try to cast him in this role. Only those who are historically "immersed" in the complex forms of oppression taken by life in the United States can identify the special garb worn by "cultural silence" in this society. Clearly it is not illiteracy, as in northeast Brazil, or economic marginalization as in rural Chile. What is it, then, that blocks oppressed Americans from controlling their own social destiny? Is it the lack of certain skills, or the inability to manipulate the law to their own ends, as the dominant classes do with impunity? Is it faulty ideology or the inability to organize locally beyond mere self-interest? Or is it because the psychic boundaries between oppressors and oppressed in the United States are so fuzzy? Do most Americans recognize themselves as either oppressed or oppressors, or do they see themselves as inert beneficiaries, and thereby passive connivers, in impersonal structures of oppression? And are racism and sexism in this society manifestations of what Freire, echoing Mao, calls the "principal contradiction" or merely, as he suggests, "principal aspects of the principal contradiction"? These and similar questions must be answered—in a dialectical way which grows from *praxis* and which generates theory—before Paulo Freire's "method" can be applied to the United States.

The futility of looking to the Freire "method" as a panacea is dramatized in this volume's second essay, "Extension or Communication." This work, written in Chile in 1968, applies the lessons of "conscientização" to a domain of vital importance in Latin America, namely, rural extension. Extension workers and county agents are familiar figures on the U.S. rural landscape; they bring advanced techniques and products developed in agricultural schools and land-grant colleges to the farmers. And in recent decades, rural extension on the U.S. model has spread throughout Latin America. In many areas, extension stands as the epitome of technical assistance. Nevertheless, as he analyzes the terms "extension" and "communication," and the realities underlying them, Freire detects a basic contradiction between the two. Genuine dialogue with peasants, he holds, is incompatible with "extending" to them technical expertise or agricultural know-how. Consequently, "Extension or Communication" cannot be read as a specialized tract of interest only to rural people. On the contrary, it has general significance precisely because it demystifies all "aid" or "helping" relationships. What the author says of extension agents he might also say of social workers, city planners, welfare administrators, community organizers, political militants, and a host of others who allegedly render "services" to the poor or the powerless.

Freire insists that methodological failings can always be traced to ideological errors. Behind the practice of agricultural extension, he sees an (implicit) ideology of paternalism, social control, and non-reciprocity between experts and "helpees." If, on the other hand, one is to adopt a *method* which fosters dialogue and reciprocity, one must first be *ideologically* committed to equality, to the abolition of privilege, and to non-elitist forms of leadership wherein special qualifications may be exercised, but are not perpetuated. In rejecting the language and practice of extensionism, therefore, Freire does not negate the value of bringing agricultural technology or skills to peasants. But he asserts that those who have such knowledge must engage in dialogue wherein they may learn, together with peasants, how to apply their common partial knowledge to the *totality* of the problematized rural situation. Implied here is the judgment, which Freire makes unequivocally, that there can be no valid "aid" and that there is no room in development language for the terms "donors" and "recipients." For this reason, therefore, "Extension or Communication" may strike readers in this country as a radical attack on U.S. foreign-aid policy and U.S. treatment of the domestic "poverty" issue. This exegesis of the oppressive character of all non-reciprocal relationships can best be read in tandem with *Pedagogy of the Oppressed* and *Cultural Action for Freedom*.

In his preface to the Spanish version of the essay, Jacques Chonchol, Minister of Agriculture in Chile's Allende government, correctly draws attention to Freire's analysis of the relations between technology and modernization. As Chonchol puts it, Freire "shows how to avoid the traditionalism of the status quo without falling into technological messianism." And both conclude that "while all development is modernization, not all modernization is development." One glimpses here the dialectic at work in Chile between the language of development and the vocabulary of liberation. This cross-fertilization is explicit in Freire's discussion of "mechanistic modernization." For him modernization is a purely mechanical process, responsive to the catalytic action of technicians, or manipulators who keep the locus of decisions outside the society undergoing change. This approach prevents that society, in short, from becoming the subject of its own transformation. But true agricultural development, like genuine land reform, requires that new structures and practices emerge from the old ones, thanks to the creativity generated by critical exchanges between "advanced technology and the empirical techniques of the peasants." As used here the term "empirical" evokes not the realm of social-science verification, but rather the world of those who live in daily familiarity with the soil: the world of trial and error, common sense and common wisdom. Hence extension agents can "communicate" only by entering the cultural universe of peasants. This they can do only by becoming vulnerable and by ratifying the reciprocity which their role as genuine educators dictates.

Freire does not minimize the obstacles faced by educators in rural settings. Nevertheless, for him the central issue faced by all change agents is: how to get results with maximum efficiency without losing time. Do dialogue and communication necessarily lead to lost time and, thereby, to delayed gains in production, so vital for national development? It would be naïve, he replies, not to strive for higher agricultural production. But such increases must find their basis in the real relationships which bind tillers of the land to nature and to their historical/cultural space. Accordingly, time is lost or efficiency is sacrificed only when peasants are "reified" by empty verbalism or by technocratic activism, both of which are enemies of true *praxis*. There-fore, each moment spent in dialogue which prepares men and women to "emerge" from their state of "immersion" is time gained. Conversely, all is lost, in spite of glittering ap-pearances, if natural objects or social structures are for-mally altered but human subjects are left powerless as be-fore. The goal of land reform, as of all developmental change, is to transform people, not merely to change struc-tures. Freire's concern for people is so central that it rules out any policy, program, or project which does not become truly *theirs*. The mark of a successful educator is not skill in persuasion—which is but an insidious form of propaganda —but the ability to dialogue with educatees in a mode of reciprocity. And rural extension fails as communication because it violates the dialectic of reciprocity; indeed no change agent or technical expert has the right to impose personal options on others.

Two final remarks apply to Freire's overall work. The first evokes his Utopian vision. Paulo Freire's Utopianism is no idealistic dream spun out of a mind ideologically en-amored of dialogue or of critical consciousness. No, it grows out of his practical involvement with oppressed groups in a process of struggle. To theorize otherwise, for Freire, is to foster a particularly repulsive form of naïve consciousness. Hence Freire cannot be taken seriously if he is judged only in terms of short-term results. The oppressed in every society have no difficulty recognizing his voice as their own, in their efforts to overcome their cultural silence. Those who are truly oppressed do not enjoy the freedom to fail, the luxury of experimenting. This is why they heed only serious ideas which they can put into practice. It is in this basic way that Freire's approach to education, commun-ication, and technology is serious: it means nothing unless it is assumed and re-created by human communities in strug-gle. Necessarily, therefore, short-term results may prove disappointing because such efforts view creative Utopianism as the only viable brand of realistic politics in a world char-acterized by the *praxis* of domination.

The second comment touches on Freire's personal style

as educator. Now that he has visited the United States on several occasions and addressed numerous audiences, one can no longer dissociate his written from his oral work. His own educational practice stands as proof that dialogue is possible, that educators can learn together with educatees. Freire stubbornly refuses to be cast in the role of a charismatic guru dispensing wisdom to willing disciples. Unless one can criticize him, one cannot exchange thoughts with him. He is ever prompt to "decree his own death as an educator" (to use his own words) whenever he meets an interlocutor who unmasks some residual *naïveté* in his own thought. The quality of his human relationships, even with total strangers, is testimony to his theory that all people are important and merit active respect. In a word, Paulo Freire is one of those rare persons whose stature grows the closer one gets to him. Increased familiarity breeds, not contempt, but a desire to read him anew with a more attentive ear. To know him is to become convinced that liberating education and authentic communication are indeed possible.

DENIS GOULET

Education for Critical Consciousness

Education as the Practice of Freedom

Translated and Edited by Myra Bergman Ramos

Society in Transition

To be human is to engage in relationships with others and with the world. It is to experience that world as an objective reality, independent of oneself, capable of being known. Animals, submerged within reality, cannot relate to it; they are creatures of mere *contacts*. But man's separateness from and openness to the world distinguishes him as a being of *relationships*. Men, unlike animals, are not only *in* the world but *with* the world.

Human relationships with the world are plural in nature. Whether facing widely different challenges of the environment or the same challenge, men are not limited to a single reaction pattern. They organize themselves, choose the best response, test themselves, act, and change in the very act of responding. They do all this consciously, as one uses a tool to deal with a problem.

Men relate to their world in a critical way. They apprehend the objective data of their reality (as well as the ties that link one datum to another) through reflection—not by reflex, as do animals. And in the act of critical perception, men discover their own temporality. Transcending a single dimension, they reach back to yesterday, recognize today, and come upon tomorrow. The dimensionality of time is one of the fundamental discoveries in the history of human culture. In illiterate cultures, the "weight" of apparently limitless time hindered people from reaching that consciousness of temporality, and thereby achieving a sense of their historical nature. A cat has no historicity; his inability to emerge from time submerges him in a totally one-dimensional "today" of which he has no consciousness. Men exist[1]

---

1. In the English language, the terms "live" and "exist" have assumed implications opposite to their etymological origins. As used here, to exist is more than to live, because it is more than being in the world; it is to be with the world as well. And this capacity for communication between the being which exists and the objective world gives to "existing" a quality of critical capacity not present in mere "living." Transcending, discerning, entering into

in time. They are inside. They are outside. They inherit. They incorporate. They modify. Men are not imprisoned within a permanent "today"; they emerge, and become temporalized.

As men emerge from time, discover temporality, and free themselves from "today," their relations with the world become impregnated with consequence. The normal role of human beings in and with the world is not a passive one. Because they are not limited to the natural (biological) sphere but participate in the creative dimension as well, men can intervene in reality in order to change it. Inheriting acquired experience, creating and re-creating, integrating themselves into their context, responding to its challenges, objectifying themselves, discerning, transcending, men enter into the domain which is theirs exclusively—that of History and of Culture.[2]

Integration with one's context, as distinguished from *adaptation,* is a distinctively human activity. Integration results from the capacity to adapt oneself to reality *plus* the critical capacity to make choices and to transform that reality. To the extent that man loses his ability to make choices and is subjected to the choices of others, to the extent that his decisions are no longer his own because they result from external prescriptions, he is no longer integrated. Rather, he has adapted. He has "adjusted." Unpliant men, with a revolutionary spirit, are often termed "maladjusted."

The integrated person is person as *Subject.* In contrast, the adaptive person is person as *object,* adaptation representing at most a weak form of self-defense. If man is incapable of changing reality, he adjusts himself instead. Adaptation is behavior characteristic of the animal sphere; exhibited by man, it is symptomatic of his dehumanization.

---

dialogue (communicating and participating) are exclusively attributes of existence. One can only exist in relation to others who also exist, and in communication with them. In this regard, see Karl Jaspers, *The Origin and Goal of History* (New Haven, 1953), and *Reason and Anti-reason in our Time* (New Haven, 1952).
2. See Erich Kahler, *Historia Universal del Hombre.*

Throughout history men have attempted to overcome the factors which make them accommodate or adjust, in a struggle—constantly threatened by oppression—to attain their full humanity.

As men relate to the world by responding to the challenges of the environment, they begin to dynamize, to master, and to humanize reality. They add to it something of their own making, by giving temporal meaning to geographic space, by creating culture. This interplay of men's relations with the world and with their fellows does not (except in cases of repressive power) permit societal or cultural immobility. As men create, re-create, and decide, historical epochs begin to take shape.[3] And it is by creating, re-creating and deciding *that men should participate* in these epochs.

An historical epoch is characterized by a series of aspirations, concerns, and values in search of fulfillment; by ways of being and behaving; by more or less generalized attitudes. The concrete representations of many of these aspirations, concerns, and values, as well as the obstacles to their fulfillment, constitute the themes of that epoch, which in turn indicate tasks to be carried out.[4] The epochs are fulfilled to the degree that their themes are grasped and their tasks solved; and they are superseded when their themes and tasks no longer correspond to newly emerging concerns.

Men play a crucial role in the fulfillment and in the superseding of the epochs. Whether or not men can perceive the epochal themes and above all, how they act upon the reality within which these themes are generated will largely determine their humanization or dehumanization, their affirmation as Subjects or their reduction as objects. For only as men grasp the themes can they intervene in reality instead of remaining mere onlookers. And only by developing a permanently critical attitude can men overcome a posture of adjustment in order to become integrated with the spirit

---

3. See Hans Freyer, *Teoría de la época atual* (Mexico).
4. See Paulo Freire, *Pedagogy of the Oppressed* (New York, 1970), pp. 91–92. (Translator's note.)

of the time. To the extent that an epoch dynamically generates its own themes, men will have to make "more and more use of intellectual, and less and less of emotional and instinctive functions. . . . "[5]

But unfortunately, what happens to a greater or lesser degree in the various "worlds" into which the world is divided is that the ordinary person is crushed, diminished, converted into a spectator, maneuvered by myths which powerful social forces have created. These myths turn against him; they destroy and annihilate him. Tragically frightened, men fear authentic relationships and even doubt the possibility of their existence. On the other hand, fearing solitude, they gather in groups lacking in any critical and loving ties which might transform them into a cooperating unit, into a true community. "Gregariousness is always the refuge of mediocrities," said Nikolai Nikolaievich Vedeniapin in *Dr. Zhivago*. It is also an imprisoning armor which prevents men from loving.

Perhaps the greatest tragedy of modern man is his domination by the force of these myths and his manipulation by organized advertising, ideological or otherwise. Gradually, without even realizing the loss, he relinquishes his capacity for choice; he is expelled from the orbit of decisions. Ordinary men do not perceive the tasks of the time; the latter are interpreted by an "elite" and presented in the form of recipes, of prescriptions. And when men try to save themselves by following the prescriptions, they drown in leveling anonymity, without hope and without faith, domesticated and adjusted.

As Erich Fromm said in *Escape from Freedom*:[6]

[Man] has become free from the external bonds that would prevent him from doing and thinking as he sees fit. He would be free to act according to his own will, if he knew what he wanted, thought, and felt. But he does not know. He conforms to anonymous authorities and adopts a self which is not his. The more he does this, the more powerless he feels, the more is he

5. Zevedei Barbu, *Democracy and Dictatorship, Their Psychology and Patterns of Life* (New York, 1956), p. 4.
6. (New York, 1960), pp. 255–256.

forced to conform. In spite of a veneer of optimism and initiative, modern man is overcome by a profound feeling of powerlessness which makes him gaze toward approaching catastrophes as though he were paralyzed.

If men are unable to perceive critically the themes of their time, and thus to intervene actively in reality, they are carried along in the wake of change. They see that the times are changing, but they are submerged in that change and so cannot discern its dramatic significance. And a society beginning to move from one epoch to another requires the development of an especially flexible, critical spirit. Lacking such a spirit, men cannot perceive the marked contradictions which occur in society as emerging values in search of affirmation and fulfillment clash with earlier values seeking self-preservation. The time of epochal transition constitutes an historical-cultural "tidal wave." Contradictions increase between the ways of being, understanding, behaving, and valuing which belong to yesterday and other ways of perceiving and valuing which announce the future. As the contradictions deepen, the "tidal wave" becomes stronger and its climate increasingly emotional. This shock between a *yesterday* which is losing relevance but still seeking to survive, and a *tomorrow* which is gaining substance, characterizes the phase of transition as a time of announcement and a time of decision. Only, however, to the degree that the choices result from a critical perception of the contradictions are they real and capable of being transformed in action. Choice is illusory to the degree it represents the expectations of others.

While all transition involves change, not all change results in transition. Changes can occur within a single historical epoch that do not profoundly affect it in any way. There is a normal interplay of social readjustments resulting from the search for fulfillment of the themes. However, when these themes begin to lose their substance and significance and new themes emerge, it is a sign that society is beginning to move into a new epoch. The time of transition involves a rapid movement in search of new themes and new tasks. In such a phase man needs more than ever to be integrated with his reality. If he lacks the capacity to perceive the "mystery" of the changes, he will be a mere pawn at their mercy.

Brazil, in the 1950s and early 1960s, was precisely in this position of moving from one epoch to another. Which were the themes and the tasks which had lost and were losing their substance in Brazilian society? All those characteristic of a "closed society."[7] For instance, Brazil's non-autonomous status had generated the theme of cultural alienation. Elite and masses alike lacked integration with Brazilian reality. The elite lived "superimposed" upon that reality; the people, submerged within it. To the elite fell the task of importing alien cultural models; to the people, the task of following, of being *under,* of being ruled by the elite, of having no task of their own.

With the split in Brazilian society, the entire complex of themes and tasks assumed a new aspect. The particular meaning and emphasis given by a closed society to themes like democracy, popular participation, freedom, property, authority, and education were no longer adequate for a society in transition. (Similarly, the military *coup* of 1964 required a new perception of the themes and tasks characteristic of the transitional phase.) If Brazil was to move surely toward becoming a homogeneously open society, the correct perception of new aspirations and a new perception of old themes were essential. Should a distortion of this perception occur, however, a corresponding distortion in the transition would lead not to an open society but toward a "massified" society[8] of adjusted and domesticated men.

Thus, in that transitional phase, education became a highly important task. Its potential force would depend above all upon our capacity to participate in the dynamism of the

---

7. See Karl Popper, *The Open Society and Its Enemies* (Princeton, 1966).
8. A "massified" society is one in which the people, after entering the historical process, have been manipulated by the elite into an unthinking, manageable agglomeration. This process is termed "massification." It stands in contrast to *conscientização,* which is the process of achieving a critical consciousness. (Translator's note.)

transitional epoch. It would depend upon our distinguishing clearly which elements truly belonged to the transition and which were simply present in it. As the link between one epoch in exhaustion and another gaining substance, the transition had aspects of prolonging and conserving the old society at the same time that it extended forward into the new society. The new perceptions did not prevail easily or without sacrifice; the old themes had to exhaust their validity before they could give way to the new. Thus the dynamic of transition involved the confusion of flux and reflux, advances and retreats. And those who lacked the ability to perceive the mystery of the times responded to each retreat with tragic hopelessness and generalized fear.

In the last analysis, retreats do not deter the transition. They do not constitute backward movement, although they can retard movement or distort it. The new themes (or new perceptions of old themes) which are repressed during the retreats will persist in their advance until such time as the validity of the old themes is exhausted and the new ones reach fulfillment. At that point, society will once more find itself in its normal rhythm of changes, awaiting a new moment of transition. Thus the moment of transition belongs much more to "tomorrow," to the new time it announces, than it does to the old.

The starting point for the Brazilian transition was that closed society to which I have already referred, one whose raw material export economy was determined by an external market, whose very center of economic decision was located abroad—a "reflex," "object" society, lacking a sense of nationhood. Backward. Illiterate. Anti-dialogical. Elitist.

That society split apart with the rupture of the forces which had kept it in equilibrium. The economic changes which began in the last century with industrialization, and which increased in this century, were instrumental in this cleavage. Brazil was a society no longer totally closed but not yet truly open: a society in the *process* of opening. The urban centers had become predominantly open, while the rural areas remained predominantly closed. Meanwhile the society ran the risk (due to the continual possibility of retreats, *viz.,* the present military regime) of a catastrophic return to closure.

The democratic salvation of Brazil would lie in making our society homogeneously open. The challenge of achieving that openness was taken up by various contradictory forces, both external and internal. Some groups truly believed that the increasing political participation of the people during the transitional epoch would make it possible to achieve an open, autonomous society without violence. Other, reactionary, forces sought at all costs to obstruct any advance and to maintain the status quo indefinitely—or worse still, to bring about a retreat. While it would be impossible to return the emerging masses to their previous state of submersion, it might be possible to lead them to immobility and silence in the name of their own freedom. Men and institutions began to divide into two general categories—reactionaries and progressives; into those men and institutions which were *in* the process of transition and those which were not only in but *of* transition. The deepening of the clash between old and new encouraged a tendency to choose one side or the other; and the emotional climate of the time encouraged the tendency to become radical about that choice.

Radicalization involves increased commitment to the position one has chosen. It is predominantly critical, loving, humble, and communicative, and therefore a positive stance. The man who has made a radical option does not deny another man's right to choose, nor does he try to impose his own choice. He can discuss their respective positions. He is convinced he is right, but respects another man's prerogative to judge himself correct. He tries to convince and convert, not to crush his opponent. The radical does, however, have the duty, imposed by love itself, to react against the violence of those who try to silence him—of those who, in the name of freedom, kill his freedom and their own.[9] To

---

9. Every relationship of domination, of exploitation, of oppression, is by definition violent, whether or not the violence is expressed by drastic means. In such a relationship, dominator and dominated alike are reduced to things —the former dehumanized by an excess of power, the latter by lack of it.

be radical does not imply self-flagellation. Radicals cannot passively accept a situation in which the excessive power of a few leads to the dehumanization of all.

Unfortunately, the Brazilian people, elite and masses alike, were generally unprepared to evaluate the transition critically; and so, tossed about by the force of the contending contradictions, they began to fall into sectarian positions instead of opting for radical solutions. Sectarianism is predominantly emotional and uncritical. It is arrogant, antidialogical and thus anticommunicative. It is a reactionary stance, whether on the part of a rightist (whom I consider a "born" sectarian) or a leftist. The sectarian creates nothing because he cannot love. Disrespecting the choices of others, he tries to impose his own choice on everyone else. Herein lies the inclination of the sectarian to activism: action without the vigilance of reflection; herein his taste for sloganizing, which generally remains at the level of myth and half-truths and attributes absolute value to the purely relative.[10] The radical, in contrast, rejects activism and submits his actions to reflection.

The sectarian, whether rightist or leftist, sets himself up as the proprietor of history, as its sole creator, and the one entitled to set the pace of its movement. Rightist and leftist sectarians do differ in that one desires to stop the course of history, the other to anticipate it. On the other hand, they are similar in imposing their own convictions on the people, whom they thereby reduce to mere masses. For the sectarian, the people matter only as a support for his own goals. The sectarian wishes the people to be present at the historical process as activists, maneuvered by intoxicating propaganda. They are not supposed to think. Someone else will think for them; and it is as protégés, as children, that

---

And things cannot love. When the oppressed legitimately rise up against their oppressor, however, it is they who are usually labelled "violent," "barbaric," "inhuman," and "cold." (Among the innumerable rights claimed by the dominating consciousness is the right to define violence, and to locate it. Oppressors never see themselves as violent.)

10. See Tristão de Ataíde, *O Existencialismo e Outros Mitos do Nosso Tempo* (Rio de Janeiro, 1956).

the sectarian sees them. Sectarians can never carry out a truly liberating revolution, because they are themselves un-free.

The radical is a Subject to the degree that he perceives historical contradictions in increasingly critical fashion; however, he does not consider himself the proprietor of history. And while he recognizes that it is impossible to stop or to anticipate history without penalty, he is no mere spectator of the historical process. On the contrary, he knows that as a Subject he can and ought, together with other Subjects, to participate creatively in that process by discerning transformations in order to aid and accelerate them.[11]

In the Brazilian transition, it was the sectarians, especially those of the right, who predominated, rather than the radicals.[12] And fanaticism flourished, fanned by the irrational climate arising as the contradictions in society deepened. This fanaticism, which separated and brutalized men, created hatred, thus threatening the essential promises of the transition—the humanization of the Brazilian people and their extraordinary sense of hope, hope rooted in the passage of Brazilian society from its previous colonial, reflex status to that of a Subject.

In alienated societies, men oscillate between ingenuous

---

11. For a further discussion of radicalization and sectarianism, see *Pedagogy of the Oppressed*, pp. 21–24. (Translator's note.)

12. At that time, radical positions in the sense I have described them were being taken principally, although not exclusively, by groups of Christians who believed with Mounier that "History," both the history of the world and the history of human beings, has meaning. (This is the first of Mounier's four fundamental ideas regarding the idea of progress as a modern theme. The second is that progress proceeds continuously, although diverse vicissitudes may complicate its course, and that its movement is the movement of man's liberation. The third idea is that the development of science and technique which characterizes the modern Western age and is spreading over the entire world constitutes a decisive aspect of this liberation. The last is that in this ascent man is charged with being the author of his own liberation. See Emanuel Mounier, "Le christianisme et la notion de Progrès," *La Petite Peur du xxe Siecle* [Paris, 1948] pp. 97–152. Irrational sectarians, including some Christians, either did not understand or did not want to understand the radicals' search for integration with Brazilian problems. They did not understand the radicals' concern with progress, leading toward human liberation. And so they accused these radicals of attempting to dehumanize the Brazilian people.

optimism and hopelessness. Incapable of autonomous projects, they seek to transplant from other cultures solutions to their problems. But since these borrowed solutions are neither generated by a critical analysis of the context itself, nor adequately adapted to the context,[13] they prove inoperative and unfruitful. Finally the older generations give in to disheartenment and feelings of inferiority. But at some point in the historical process of these societies, new facts occur which provoke the first attempts at self-awareness, whereupon a new cultural climate begins to form. Some previously alienated intellectual groups begin to integrate themselves with their cultural reality. Entering the world, they perceive the old themes anew and grasp the tasks of their time. Bit by bit, these groups begin to see themselves and their society from their own perspective; they become aware of their own potentialities. This is the point at which hopelessness begins to be replaced by hope. Thus, nascent hope coincides with an increasingly critical perception of the concrete conditions of reality. Society now reveals itself as something unfinished, not as something inexorably given; it has become a challenge rather than a hopeless limitation. This new, critical optimism requires a strong sense of social responsibility and of engagement in the task of transforming society; it cannot mean simply letting things run on.

But the climate of hope is adversely affected by the impact of sectarianism, which arises as the split in the closed society leads to the phenomenon Mannheim has called "fundamental democratization." This democratization, opening like a fan into interdependent dimensions (economic, social, political, and cultural), characterized the unprecedented participating presence of the Brazilian people in the phase of transition. During the phase of the closed society, the people are *submerged* in reality. As that society breaks open, they *emerge*. No longer *mere spectators,* they uncross their arms, renounce expectancy, and demand intervention. No longer satisfied to watch, they want to participate. This

---

13. See Alberto Guerreiro Ramos, *A Redução Sociológica* (Rio de Janeiro, 1958).

participation disturbs the privileged elite, who band together in self-defense.

At first, the elite react spontaneously. Later, perceiving more clearly the threat involved in the awakening of popular consciousness, they organize. They bring forth a group of "crisis theoreticians" (the new cultural climate is usually labelled a crisis); they create social assistance institutions and armies of social workers; and—in the name of a supposedly threatened freedom—they repel the participation of the people.

The elite defend a *sui generis* democracy, in which the people are "unwell" and require "medicine"—whereas in fact their "ailment" is the wish to speak up and participate. Each time the people try to express themselves freely and to act, it is a sign they continue to be ill and thus need more medicine. In this strange interpretation of democracy, health is synonymous with popular silence and inaction. The defenders of this "democracy" speak often of the need to protect the people from what they call "foreign ideologies" —i.e., anything that could contribute to the active presence of the people in their own historical process. Similarly, they label as "subversives" all those who enter into the dynamics of the transition and become its representatives. "These people are subversive" (we are told) "because they threaten order." Actually, the elite have no alternative. As the dominant social class, they must preserve at all costs the social "order" in which they are dominant. They cannot permit any basic changes which would affect their control over decision-making. So from their point of view, every effort to supersede such an order means to subvert it criminally.

During the Brazilian transition, as the popular classes renounced a position of accommodation and claimed their right to participate actively in the historical process, reactionary groups saw clearly the resulting threat to their interests. To end this uncomfortable quandary, they needed —in addition to the power they already possessed—the government, which at least in part they did not possess. Eventually, a *coup d' état* was to solve that problem.

In such an historical-cultural climate, it is virtually impossible for intensely emotional forces not to be unleashed. This irrational climate bred and nourished sectarian positions on the part of those who wished to stop history in order to maintain their own privileges, and of those who hoped to anticipate history in order to "end" privileges. Both positions contributed to the massification and the relegation of the Brazilian people, who had only just begun to become a true "people." Misunderstood and caught in the middle (though they were not centrists) were the radicals, who wanted solutions to be found *with* the people, not *for* them or *superimposed upon* them. Radicals rejected the palliatives of "assistencialism,"[14] the force of decrees, and the irrational fanaticism of "crusades," instead defending basic transformations in society which would treat men as persons and thus as Subjects. Internal reactionary forces centered around latifundiary[15] interests were joined and given support by external forces that wished to prevent Brazil's transformation from an object to a Subject society. These external forces attempted their own pressures and their own assistencial solutions.

Assistencialism is an especially pernicious method of trying to vitiate popular participation in the historical process. In the first place, it contradicts man's natural vocation as Subject in that it treats the recipient as a passive object, incapable of participating in the process of his own recuperation; in the second place, it contradicts the process of "fundamental democratization." The greatest danger of assistencialism is the violence of its anti-dialogue, which by imposing silence and passivity denies men conditions likely to develop or to "open" their consciousness. For without an increasingly critical consciousness men are not able to integrate themselves into a transitional society, marked by

---

14. Assistencialism: a term used in Latin America to describe policies of financial or social assistance which attack symptoms, but not causes, of social ills.
15. *Latifundium:* a noun of Latin origin which, in Spanish and Portuguese, means a large privately owned landholding. (Translator's note.)

intense change and contradictions. Assistencialism is thus both an effect and a cause of massification.

The important thing is to help men (and nations) help themselves,[16] to place them in consciously critical confrontation with their problems, to make them the agents of their own recuperation. In contrast, assistencialism robs men of a fundamental human necessity—responsibility, of which Simone Weil says:

For this need to be satisfied it is necessary that a man should often have to take decisions in matters great or small affecting interests that are distinct from his own, but in regard to which he feels a personal concern.[17]

Responsibility cannot be acquired intellectually, but only through experience. Assistencialism offers no responsibility, no opportunity to make decisions, but only gestures and attitudes which encourage passivity. Whether the assistance is of foreign or national origin, this method cannot lead a country to a democratic destination.

Brazil in transition needed urgently to find rapid and sure solutions to its distressing problems—but *solutions with the people and never for them or imposed upon them.* What was needed was to go to the people and help them to enter the historical process critically. The prerequisite for this task was a form of education enabling the people to reflect on themselves, their responsibilities, and their role in the new cultural climate—indeed to reflect on their very *power* of reflection. The resulting development of this power would mean an increased capacity for choice. Such an education would take into the most serious account the various levels at which the Brazilian people perceived their reality, as being of the greatest importance for the process

---

16. Speaking of the relations between rich and poor nations, developed and developing nations, Pope John XXIII urged the rich not to aid the poor by means of what he termed "disguised forms of colonial domination." Rather, he said, aid should be given without self-interest, with the sole intention of making it possible for nations to develop themselves economically and socially. Assistencialism cannot do this, for it is precisely one of those forms of colonial domination. See "Christianity and Social Progress," from the Encyclical Letter *Mater et Magistra,* articles 171 and 172.

17. *The Need for Roots* (New York, 1952), p. 15.

of their humanization. Therein lay my own concern to analyze these historically and culturally conditioned levels of
understanding.

Men submerged in the historical process are characterized
by a state I have described as "semi-intransitivity of consciousness."[18] It is the consciousness of men belonging to
what Fernando de Azevedo has called "circumscribed" and
"introverted" communities,[19] the consciousness which prevailed in the closed Brazilian society and which predomi-
nates even today in the most backward regions of Brazil.
Men of semi-intransitive consciousness cannot apprehend
problems situated outside their sphere of biological necessity. Their interests center almost totally around survival,
and they lack a sense of life on a more historic plane. The
concept of semi-intransitivity does not signify the closure of
a person within himself, crushed by an all-powerful time and
space. Whatever his state, man is an open being. Rather,
semi-intransitive consciousness means that his sphere of perception is limited, that he is impermeable to challenges
situated outside the sphere of biological necessity. In this
sense only, semi-intransitivity represents a near disengagement between men and their existence. In this state, discern-
ment is difficult. Men confuse their perceptions of the objects and challenges of the environment, and fall prey to
magical explanations because they cannot apprehend true
causality.

As men amplify their power to perceive and respond to
suggestions and questions arising in their context, and increase their capacity to enter into dialogue not only with
other men but with their world, they become "transitive."
Their interests and concerns now extend beyond the simple
vital sphere. Transitivity of consciousness makes man "permeable." It leads him to replace his disengagement from
existence with almost total engagement. Existence is a dy-

---

18. This theme is treated in greater detail in my *Cultural Action for Freedom*, Monograph Series No. 7, 1970, Harvard Educational Review, Center
for the Study of Development and Social Change.
19. *Educaçao entre Dois Mundos* (São Paulo), p. 34.

namic concept, implying eternal dialogue between man and man, between man and the world, between man and his Creator. It is this dialogue which makes of man an historical being.

There is, however, an initial, predominantly naïve, stage of transitive consciousness. *Naïve transitivity*, the state of consciousness which predominated in Brazilian urban centers during the transitional period, is characterized by an over-simplification of problems; by a nostalgia for the past; by underestimation of the common man; by a strong tendency to gregariousness; by a lack of interest in investigation, accompanied by an accentuated taste for fanciful explanations; by fragility of argument; by a strongly emotional style; by the practice of polemics rather than dialogue; by magical explanations. (The magical aspect typical of intransitivity is partially present here also. Although men's horizons have expanded and they respond more openly to stimuli, these responses still have a magical quality.) Naïve transitivity is the consciousness of men who are still almost part of a mass, in whom the developing capacity for dialogue is still fragile and capable of distortion. If this consciousness does not progress to the stage of *critical transitivity*, it may be deflected by sectarian irrationality into fanaticism.

The critically transitive consciousness is characterized by depth in the interpretation of problems; by the substitution of causal principles for magical explanations; by the testing of one's "findings" and by openness to revision; by the attempt to avoid distortion when perceiving problems and to avoid preconceived notions when analyzing them; by refusing to transfer responsibility; by rejecting passive positions; by soundness of argumentation; by the practice of dialogue rather than polemics; by receptivity to the new for reasons beyond mere novelty and by the good sense not to reject the old just because it is old—by accepting what is valid in both old and new. Critical transitivity is characteristic of authentically democratic regimes and corresponds to highly permeable, interrogative, restless and dialogical forms of life—in contrast to silence and inaction, in contrast to the rigid, militarily authoritarian state presently prevailing in Brazil, an historical retreat which the usurpers of power try to present as a reencounter with democracy.

There are certain positions, attitudes, and gestures associated with the awakening of critical awareness, which occur naturally due to economic progress. These should not be confused with an authentically critical position, which a person must make his own by intervention in and integration with his own context. *Conscientização* represents the *development* of the awakening of critical awareness. It will not appear as a natural byproduct of even major economic changes, but must grow out of a critical educational effort based on favorable historical conditions.

In Brazil, the passage from a predominantly intransitive consciousness to a predominantly naïve transitivity paralleled the transformation of economic patterns. As the process of urbanization intensified, men were thrust into more complex forms of life. As men entered a larger sphere of relationships and received a greater number of suggestions and challenges to their circumstances, their consciousness automatically became more transitive. However, the further, crucial step from naïve transitivity to critical transitivity would *not* occur automatically. Achieving this step would thus require an active, dialogical educational program concerned with social and political responsibility, and prepared to avoid the danger of massification.

There is a close potential relationship between naïve transitivity and massification. If a person does not move from naïve transitivity to a critical consciousness but instead falls into a *fanaticized consciousness*,[27] he will become even more disengaged from reality than in the semi-intransitive state. To the extent that a person acts more on the basis of emotionality than of reason,[28] his behavior occurs adaptively and cannot result in commitment, for committed behavior

---

27. See Gabriel Marcel, *Man Against Mass Society* (Chicago, 1962).
28. Barbu sees reason as "the individual capacity to grasp the order in change, and the unity in variety." *Op cit.,* p. 4.

has its roots in critical consciousness and capacity for genuine choice. The adaptation and lack of engagement typical of semi-intransitivity are thus more prevalent still in a state of massification. The power to perceive authentic causality is obliterated in the semi-intransitive state; hence the latter's *magical* quality. In massification this power is distorted, producing a *mythical* quality. In the semi-intransitive state, men are predominantly *illogical;* in fanaticized consciousness the distortion of reason makes men *irrational.* The possibility of dialogue diminishes markedly. Men are defeated and dominated, though they do not know it; they fear freedom, though they believe themselves to be free. They follow general formulas and prescriptions as if by their own choice. They are directed; they do not direct themselves. Their creative power is impaired. They are objects, not Subjects. For men to overcome their state of massification, they must be enabled to reflect about that very condition. But since authentic reflection cannot exist apart from action, men must also act to transform the concrete reality which has determined their massification.

In short, naïve transitive consciousness can evolve toward critical transitivity, characteristic of a legitimately democratic mentality, or it can be deflected toward the debased, clearly dehumanized, fanaticized consciousness characteristic of massification. During the Brazilian transition, as the emotional climate became more intense and sectarian irrationality (especially of the right) grew stronger, there was increasing resistance to an educational program capable of helping the people move from ingenuity to criticism. Indeed, if the people were to become critical, enter reality, increase their capacity to make choices (and therefore their capacity to reject the prescriptions of others), the threat to privilege would increase as well. To irrational sectarians, the humanization of the Brazilian people loomed as the specter of their own dehumanization, and any effort toward this end as subversive action. But such an effort was imperative, for those who believed that the destiny of men is to become authentic human beings.

Closed Society and
Democratic Inexperience

To understand the Brazilian transition, its advances and retreats, and its significance as the "announcement" of a new epoch, one must look at the closed, colonial, slavocratic, reflex, anti-democratic society which served as its starting point. One of the strongest characteristics of that society, always present and ready to flower in the ebbs and flows of the historical process, was our lack of democratic experience. This lack has been and continues to be one of the major obstacles to our democratization—not an insurmountable barrier, but neither one to be underestimated. To cite an apparently obvious but absolutely fundamental warning: "Mind in all its manifestations is never only what it is, but also what it was . . ."[1]

Most analysts of Brazilian history and culture have noted the absence of the preconditions for the development of participatory behavior by which we might have constructed our society "with our own hands." Experience in self-government might have afforded us an exercise in democracy; but the conditions of our colonization did not favor this possibility. In fact, Brazil developed under conditions which were hostile to the acquisition of democratic experience, with head bowed, in fear of the Crown, without a press, foreign relations, schools, or a voice of her own. Our colonization, strongly predatory, was based on economic exploitation of the large landholding and on slave labor—at first native, then African. A colonization of this type could not create conditions necessary for the development of the permeable, flexible mentality characteristic of a democratic cultural climate. Referring to the lack of political experience of the lower classes in Brazil, Caio Prado has affirmed that the "national economy, and our social organization as well,

1. Barbu, *op. cit.*, p. 9.

built as they were upon a base of slavery, could not admit of a democratic and popular political structure."[2]

At the outset, the colonization of Brazil was above all a commercial enterprise. Portugal had no intention of creating a civilization in her new lands; she was interested only in a profitable business venture. And so for years Brazil, who could offer nothing compared to the magnificence of the Eastern territories, was disdained by Portugal and left to the gluttonous incursions of adventurers. On the other hand, during the period of the Brazilian conquest, Portugal had insufficient population to engage in projects of settlement. Unfortunately for our development, the first colonizers of Brazil lacked a sense of *integration with the colony*. They wished only to exploit it, not to cultivate it; to be "over" it, not to stay in it and with it.[3] Later, contingencies arose which required actual settlement rather than mere trading posts, resulting in a greater integration of the colonizers with the land. Even then, those who came to the tropics tended to be men possessing sufficient means to establish a lucrative business; only against their will did men come as workers.

In addition (and possibly in part due to the above tendency), our colonization developed on the basis of large landholding—namely the plantation (*fazenda*) and the sugar mill (*engenho*). Immense tracts of land were granted to a single person, who took possession as well of the men who came to live and work there. On these widely separated holdings, the inhabitants had no alternative but to become protégés of their all-powerful masters. They needed protection against the predatory incursions of the natives, the arrogant violence of the tropics, the raids of other *senhores*. These conditions bred the habits of domination and dependence which still prevail among us in the form of paternalistic approaches to problems.

---

2. *Evolução Política do Brasil e Outros Estudos* (São Paulo, 1953), p. 64.
3. See the excellent study by Clodomir V. Moog, *Bandeirantes and Pioneers* (New York, 1964) in which he compares Brazilian and North American cultural development.

The enormous size of the estates, the small population of the mother country which hindered attempts at settlement, the commercial spirit of the colonization, all led to the institution of slavery. That fact created a series of obstacles to the formation of a democratic mentality, of a permeable consciousness. Antonil has given us a vivid picture of the master-slave mentality which did prevail on the *fazenda*:

Anyone who gains the title of *senhor* seems to want everyone else to behave as servants... In Brazil people say that the slave needs three "P's": *pau, pão e pano* (cudgel, bread and cloth). The phrase begins badly, with punishment, but would God that eating and clothing were as abundant as the punishment which so often is given for the slightest offense.[4]

The large estates, with highly self-sufficient economies, functioned as closed systems with a climate favoring despotism, decrees, and the "law" of the master.

In truth, there are laws which impose certain limits to the will and the ire of the masters, such as that which fixes the number of whiplashes it is permitted to inflict at one time to a slave without the intervention of the authorities; however, as I have said before, these laws are without force and perhaps are even unknown to the majority of the slaves and masters. On the other hand, the authorities are located so far distant that in reality, the punishment of a slave for a real or imaginary fault and the bad treatment resulting from the caprice and the cruelty of the master are limited only by the fear of losing the slave through death or through flight, or by respect for public opinion.[5]

The excess of power which has characterized our culture from the start created on the one hand an almost masochistic desire to submit to that power and on the other a desire to be all-powerful.[6] This habit of submission led men to *adapt* and *adjust* to their circumstances, instead of seeking to integrate themselves with reality. Integration, the behavior characteristic of flexibly democratic regimes, requires a maximum capacity for critical thought. In contrast, the adapted man, neither dialoguing nor participating, ac-

---

4. Andre João Antonil, *Engenho Real,* p. 55.
5. Johann Moritz Rugendas, *Viagem Pitoresca Através do Brasil* (São Paulo, 1940), p. 185.
6. See Gilberto Freyre, *The Masters and the Slaves* (New York, 1964).

commodates to conditions imposed upon him and thereby acquires an authoritarian and acritical frame of mind.

The social distance characteristic of human relationships on the great estate did not permit dialogue. Even the more humane relationships between masters and slaves which prevailed on some estates produced not dialogue but paternalism, the patronizing attitude of an adult towards a child.

The proper climate for dialogue is found in open areas, where men can develop a sense of participation in a common life. Dialogue requires social and political responsibility; it requires at least a minimum of transitive consciousness, which cannot develop under the closed conditions of the large estate. Herein lie the roots of Brazilian "mutism"; societies which are denied dialogue in favor of decrees become predominantly "silent."[7] (It should be noted that silence does not signify an absence of response, but rather a response which lacks a critical quality.)

Without dialogue, self-government cannot exist; hence, self-government was almost unknown among us. There was nothing in Brazil to compare to the European agrarian communities studied by Joaquim Costa, who affirmed: "Since its origins, all of European humanity has evolved under a regime of political experience."[8] In contrast, the center of gravity in Brazilian private and public life was located in external power and authority. Men were crushed by the power of the landlords, the governors, the captains, the viceroys. Introjecting this external authority, the people developed a consciousness which "housed" oppression,[9] rather than the free and creative consciousness indispensable to authentically democratic regimes. Brazil never experienced that sense of community, of participation in the solution of

---

7. I have returned to this point in more recent studies, with a preliminary analysis of what I call "the culture of silence." See particularly *Cultural Action for Freedom*.

8. "Coletivismo Agrário en España," cited by Francisco José de Oliveira Viana, *Instituições Políticas Brasileiras* (Rio de Janeiro, 1949), Vol. IV, Ch. IV.

9. For further development of this theme, see *Pedagogy of the Oppressed*, Chapter 1 (Translator's note).

common problems, which is instilled in the popular consciousness and transformed into a knowledge of democracy. On the contrary, the circumstances of our colonization and settlement created in us an extremely individualistic outlook. As Vieira said so well, "Each family is a republic."[10] Even the political solidarity of men to their landholding masters, later necessitated by the importation of political democracy, was more apparent than real.

Urban centers created and governed by the people might have afforded us an apprenticeship in democracy. But the economic organization of the country on the basis of the dispersed, self-contained landholdings did not permit the development of cities with a middle class possessing a reasonable economic base.[11] In Brazil, urban centers rarely arose out of political solidarity, out of the need to associate human groups into communities. The history of our political institutions reveals instead the pattern of creating urban nuclei by decree and of "drafting" their inhabitants. It was impossible for democratically urban life to flourish in the poverty-stricken cities, which were absorbed and suffocated by the overwhelming economic power of the great estates.

In addition, during the Colonial period Portugal maintained Brazil in almost total isolation. Drastic restrictions were imposed not only on foreign relations, but even on relations among Brazilian provinces themselves. Such relations, if permitted, would have provided an indispensable exchange of experiences by which human groups, through mutual observation, correct and improve themselves. Instead, the isolated colony was forced to satisfy the increasingly gluttonous demands of the mother country. The point is not whether the colonial policy could have been open,

---

10. As cited in Viana, *op. cit.*, Vol. I, p. 151.

11. "During this time [the 16th to the 19th century] Brazil was a society that lacked almost all forms or expressions of individual or family status except the two extremes: master and slave. The rise, to any considerable degree, of the middle class, the small independent farmer, the tradesman, is so recent among us that during that entire period it can practically be ignored." Gilberto Freyre, *The Mansion and the Shanties* (New York, 1963), p. xvi.

permeable, and democratic; it is that the excessively tutelary
nature of that policy did not permit us any democratic experience.[12] As Berlink has noted,

> In Brazil democratic aspirations have been almost nonexistent. Such was the
> submission in which the Portuguese Metropolis raised us, such was the aping
> of colonial methods by those who governed after Independence, that even
> today such aspirations are only incipient.[13]

It might be said that our Colonial municipal councils and
senates afforded some opportunity for democratic experience. But the people did not participate in these assemblies.
A privileged class governed the municipalities: the so-called
"gentlemen" whose names were inscribed in the books of the
nobility. These men were the representatives of the sugar
aristocracy, the powerful landowners, the highborn, as well
as the *nouveau riche* of the epoch, who had prospered in
commerce and been promoted to the nobility. Common men
were excluded from the elective process, and forbidden to
enter into the destiny of their communities.

So without civic rights, the people were set aside, irre-
mediably removed from any experience of self-government
or dialogue. Indeed, on occasion the people were capable of
mutiny, which is the "voice" of those who have been silent
in the creation and development of their communities. But
for the most part they were marked by submission. The
people adapted to a rigidly authoritarian structure of life,
which formed and strengthened an anti-democratic mentality.

Until special circumstances[14] were to alter the pace of
that life. In 1808 Dom João VI of Portugal arrived in Rio
de Janeiro, where he installed himself with all his Court.
The presence among us of the royal family, and especially
the transfer of the Portuguese government to Rio de

---

12. Portuguese policy toward Brazil did contain some positive aspects, such
as miscegenation, which predisposed us toward a type of "ethnic democracy."
13. Berlink, *Fatôres Adversos na Formação Brasileira.*
14. In 1807 France invaded Portugal. The Portuguese royal family fled to
Brazil and established Rio de Janeiro as the capital of Portugal (Translator's note).

Janeiro, inevitably provoked profound changes in Brazilian life. On the one hand, these changes afforded—at least to free men—new possibilities for experiences in democracy. (Paradoxically, as we shall see, these changes were also to reinforce our previous, anti-democratic traditions.)

A series of reforms following upon the arrival of the Portuguese court encouraged urban industry and activity and established schools, press, libraries, and technical education. The cities grew in power, as the rural nobility declined. In the words of Gilberto Freyre,

With the arrival of Dom João VI... the rural patriarchy, firmly established in its plantations and ranch houses—the plump ladies in the kitchen making sweets, the men puffed up with their titles and privileges of sergeant-major or captain-major, their silver goblets, spurs, and daggers, their many legitimate children and by-blows scattered about the house and the slave quarters —began to lose its grandeur of colonial days. A grandeur which the discovery of the gold mines was already undermining.[15]

This transfer of power to the cities, which began to assume a newly active position in the national life, did not as yet signify participation by the common man in the life of his community.[16] The strength of the cities lay in the opulent bourgeoisie which had prospered in commerce. Later, that strength would lie also in the ideas of the University graduates—of rural origin, but true urbanites—who had studied in Europe. These ideas were discussed in our "illiterate" provinces as if they were European centers.

But accompanying this surge of reforms and changes, and in opposition to the tenuous possibilities of democratization which might have arisen with city life, Brazil was subjected to Europeanization (or re-Europeanization), together with a series of anti-democratic procedures which reinforced our lack of democratic experience.

---

15. Freyre, *The Mansion and the Shanties,* p. 3.
16. The truly tremendous changes I have described did not yet affect the survival of slavery. That institution still impeded the new surges of development which a free labor system would later stimulate by promoting the people from a state of submission to that of at least incipient participation. Only with the split in Brazilian society and its entry into the phase of transition can one speak of a truly popular impetus.

Parallel with the process of Europeanization or re-Europeanization of Brazil, there came an intensification of the old system of oppression not only of slaves and servants by the masters, of the poor by the rich, but of Africans and natives by those who considered themselves the surrogates of European culture, that is to say, the leading city residents.... The right to gallop or canter through the streets of the cities was the prerogative of officers and militiamen, the prerogative of men dressed and shod in European style ... it was forbidden in the city of Recife, as of December 10, 1831, "to shout, scream, or cry out in the streets," a restriction directed against the Africans and their outbursts of a religious or festive nature.[17]

And it was upon this vast lack of democratic experience, characterized by a feudal mentality and sustained by a colonial economic and social structure, that we attempted to inaugurate a formal democracy. Acting in accord with our state of cultural alienation, we turned to societies we considered superior to ours in search of a prefabricated solution for our own problems. And so we imported the structure of the national democratic state without first considering our own context, unaware that the inauthenticity of superimposed solutions dooms them to failure. Not only did we lack experience in self-government when we imported the democratic state; more importantly, we were not yet able to offer the people either the circumstances or the climate for their first experiments in democracy. Upon a feudal economic structure and a social structure within which men were defeated, crushed and silenced, we superimposed a social and political form which required dialogue, participation, political and social responsibility, as well as a degree of social and political solidarity which we had not yet attained. (We had reached only the level of private solidarity, demonstrated by such manifestations as the *mutirão*.)[18]

And which of our historical conditions might have produced a genuinely popular, permeable, and critical consciousness upon which Brazil could authentically have founded a democratic state? Our feudal economic structure? The total power of the landholding masters? Our exaggerated habit

---

17. Freyre, *The Mansions and the Shanties,* p. 263, pp. 260–261.
18. *Mutirão:* a type of "work party" among friends to get a large job done quickly (Translator's note).

of submission and obedience? The absence of dialogue? The force of the various governors and officials? The lack of attention to popular education? The artificially created urban centers? The self-sufficiency of the great estate, which suffocated urban life? The prejudice against manual or mechanical labor which we inherited from slavery? Our external and internal isolation as a colony? The innumerable prohibitions against any industrial production that might affect the interests of the mother country? The Colonial municipal councils, in which common men could not participate? The growing strength of the bourgeoisie who assumed the power of the decadent rural aristocracy?

Obviously these conditions did not constitute the cultural climate necessary for the rise of democratic regimes. Before it becomes a political form, democracy is a form of life, characterized above all by a strong component of transitive consciousness. Such transitivity can neither appear nor develop except as men are launched into debate, participating in the examination of common problems. Of de Tocqueville's affirmation that a democratic reform, or democratic action in general, has to "be brought about not only with the assent of the people, but by their hand," Barbu comments:

In order to make their society "by their hand" the members of a group have to possess considerable experience in, and knowledge of, public administration. They need also certain institutions which allow them to take a share in the making of their society. But they need something more than this; they need a specific *frame of mind,* that is, certain experiences, attitudes, prejudices and beliefs shared by them all, or by a large majority.[19]

Until the split in Brazilian society offered the first conditions for popular participation, precisely the opposite situation prevailed: popular alienation, silence, and inaction. With few exceptions, the people remained at the margin of historical events or were led to those events demagogically.[20]

---

19. Barbu, *op. cit.,* p. 13.
20. The Brazilian people watched the proclamation of the Republic "in bewilderment" (Aristides Lobo), and in bewilderment they have observed the

Then, finally, major economic changes began to affect the system of forces which had maintained the closed society in equilibrium; with the end of that equilibrium, society split open and entered the phase of transition.

The first of these changes occurred toward the end of the last century. Following restrictions on the slave trade in 1850 and the abolition of slavery in 1888, capital intended for the purchase of slaves suddenly found itself without application. Little by little, this capital was employed in incipient industrial activities. Suppression of the slave trade thus led to our first attempts at internal economic growth. Further, the government policy of encouraging immigration to replace slave labor greatly stimulated our development.

At no period of the nineteenth century after Independence were there prepared and produced so many important events for the life of the nation as in the last quarter of that century ... meanwhile, the beginning of the industrial upsurge in 1885, the vigorous civilizing movement that we owe to immigration; the suppression of the slave regime which, even when carried on rapidly, as in the United States, coincided with a great increase in production, and the new economy of free labor, contributed to the transformation of the social and economic structure, which could not be without effect upon habits and mentalities, especially in the urban population.[21]

It was in this century, however, beginning in the 1920s and increasing after the Second World War, that Brazilian industrialization received its strongest impulse. At the same time, the more urbanized areas of the country grew rapidly. (It should be noted that urban growth is not always synonymous with industrial development; a Brazilian sociologist once commented that the rise of certain cities revealed more "swelling" than development.)

The above changes did indeed affect our entire national life. Culture, the arts, literature, and science showed new

---

most recent retreats in their historical process. (They are less bewildered, perhaps, with regard to the military *coup* of 1964, as the people begin to understand that historical retreats occur precisely because of their own advances. They begin to understand that it was their own growing participation in Brazilian political events, threatening the privileges of the elite, which frightened that elite into such drastic action.)

21. Fernando de Azevedo, *Brazilian Culture* (New York, 1950), pp. 409–410.

tendencies toward research, identification with Brazilian reality, and the planning of solutions rather than their importation. (The Superintendency of Development of the Northeast [SUDENE], directed by the economist Celso Furtado before the military *coup*, was an example of such planning.) The country had begun to find itself. The people emerged and began to participate in the historical process.

Education versus Massification

From the start of the Brazilian transition, it became essential to achieve economic development as a support for democracy, thereby ending the oppressive power of the rich over the very poor. This development would necessarily be autonomous and national in character. It could not limit itself to technical questions or "pure" economic policy or structural reform, but would also have to involve the passage from one mentality to another: the support of basic reforms as a foundation for development, and development as a foundation for democracy itself.

The special contribution of the educator to the birth of the new society would have to be a critical education which could help to form critical attitudes, for the naïve consciousness with which the people had emerged into the historical process left them an easy prey to irrationality. Only an education facilitating the passage from naïve to critical transitivity, increasing men's ability to perceive the challenges of their time, could prepare the people to resist the emotional power of the transition.

For as the people emerge into a state of awareness, they discover that the elite regard them with contempt;[1] in reaction, they tend whenever possible to respond aggressively. The elite, in turn, frightened at the threat to the legitimacy of their power, attempt by force or by paternalism to silence and domesticate the masses; they try to impede the process of popular emergence. These circumstances exacerbate the prevailing irrational climate, stimulating sectarian

---

1. Seymour Lipset has commented, "The poorer a country and the lower the absolute standard of living of the lower classes, the greater the pressure on the upper strata to treat the lower as vulgar, innately inferior, a lower caste beyond the pale of human society. The sharp difference in the style of living between those at the top and those at the bottom makes this psychologically necessary. Consequently, the upper strata in such a situation tend to regard political rights for the lower strata, particularly the right to share power, as essentially absurd and immoral." *Political Man* (New York, 1960), p. 66.

positions of various casts. And in large part the people, emerging but disorganized, illiterate and semi-literate, naïve and unprepared, become pawns of that irrationality. The middle class, fearing proletarization and always seeking privileges and upward mobility, view this popular emergence as, at the very least, a threat to their own "peace" and react with predictable mistrust.

The more the Brazilian transition moved toward irrational positions, the more urgently we needed to create an educational process encouraging critical attitudes. A society like ours, undergoing profound, often abrupt, changes that stimulated popular participation in the national life required a reform not only of pedagogical institutions but of the organization and educational aspects of other institutions as well, in order to effect a total approach to social and political responsibility and decision.

Karl Mannheim has said:

> ... In a society in which the main changes are to be brought about through collective deliberation, and in which re-evaluations should be based upon intellectual insight and consent, a completely new system of education would be necessary, one which would focus its main energies on the development of our intellectual powers and bring about a frame of mind which can bear the burden of scepticism and which does not panic when many of the thought habits are doomed to vanish.[2]

Although Brazil had not yet entered a phase in which "the main changes [were] made by collective deliberation," it was moving in that direction—if the phenomenon of popular participation did not regress by becoming more emotional than critical.

The education our situation demanded would enable men to discuss courageously the problems of their context—and to intervene in that context; it would warn men of the dangers of the time and offer them the confidence and the strength to confront those dangers instead of surrendering their sense of self through submission to the decisions of others. By predisposing men to reevaluate constantly, to

---

2. *Diagnosis of Our Time* (London, 1943), p. 23.

analyze "findings," to adopt scientific methods and processes, and to perceive themselves in dialectical relationship with their social reality, that education could help men to assume an increasingly critical attitude toward the world and so to transform it.

Certainly we could not rely on the mere process of technological modernization to lead us from a naïve to a critical consciousness. Indeed, an analysis of highly technological societies usually reveals the "domestication" of man's critical faculties by a situation in which he is massified and has only the illusion of choice.[3] Excluded from the sphere of decisions being made by fewer and fewer people, man is maneuvered by the mass media to the point where he believes nothing he has not heard on the radio, seen on television, or read in the newspapers.[4] He comes to accept mythical explanations of his reality. Like a man who has lost his address, he is "uprooted." Our new education would have to offer man the means to resist the "uprooting" tendencies of our industrial civilization which accompany its capacity to improve living standards.

In our highly technical world, mass production as an organization of human labor is possibly one of the most potent instruments of man's massification. By requiring a man to behave mechanically, mass production domesticates him. By separating his activity from the total project, requiring no total critical attitude toward production, it dehumanizes him. By excessively narrowing a man's specialization, it constricts his horizons, making of him a passive, fearful, naïve being. And therein lies the chief contradiction of mass production: while amplifying man's sphere of participation it simultaneously distorts this amplification by reducing man's critical capacity through exaggerated specialization.

One cannot solve this contradiction by defending outmoded and inadequate patterns of production, but by accepting reality and attempting to solve its problems objec-

---

3. By this I do not mean to say that technology is, of itself, *necessarily* massifying.
4. See C. Wright Mills, *The Power Elite* (New York, 1956).

tively. The answer does not lie in rejection of the machine, but rather in the humanization of man.[5]

Our attempt at democracy, already strongly marked by our lack of experience in self-government, was thus further threatened by the difficulties of finding our way from the prevailing state of naïve consciousness to some understanding of the significance of the rapid changes in society. For that consciousness could not give the people the conviction of participating in those changes—a conviction indispensable to the development of democracy.

In seeking to redirect our educational practice toward the goal of an authentic democracy we could ignore neither our paternalistic cultural traditions nor the new conditions of the transition. After all, these conditions were for the most part, if not distorted by irrationality, favorable to the development of a democratic mentality, since periods of accelerated change are usually attended by a greater flexibility in men's understanding, which may predispose them toward more plastic, democratic forms of life.[6]

Brazil was experiencing just such a period of change in its larger centers, from which radio, cinema, television, highway, and air transport carried influences of renewal to the smaller, more backward centers. The corresponding new transitivity of consciousness was accompanied by the phenomenon of popular rebellion. The new stimuli characteristic of an "opening" society generate a complex of activist mental attitudes. However, the somewhat abrupt emergence of the people from their previous stage of submersion leaves them more or less perplexed by the new experience of participation; and their activism takes the naïve and highly emotional form of rebellion. (The reading of Barbu is basic to the understanding of this phenomenon.)

I considered that attitude of rebellion as one of the most promising aspects of our political life—not because I espoused it as a form of action, but because it represented a

---

5. On this topic, I recommend the valuable analysis of Emanuel Mounier, *Be Not Afraid, Studies in Personalist Sociology* (New York, 1954).
6. See Barbu, *op. cit.*

symptom of advancement, an introduction to a more complete humanity. For that very reason, it could not be allowed to remain at the predominantly emotional level. My sympathy for the new activism was joined to a recognition of the need to progress from naïve rebellion to critical intervention.

I was convinced that the Brazilian people could learn social and political responsibility only by *experiencing* that responsibility, through intervention in the destiny of their children's schools, in the destinies of their trade unions and places of employment through associations, clubs, and councils, and in the life of their neighborhoods, churches, and rural communities by actively participating in associations, clubs, and charitable societies.

They could be helped to learn democracy through the *exercise* of democracy; for that knowledge, above all others, can only be assimilated experientially. More often than not, we have attempted to transfer that knowledge to the people verbally, as if we could give lessons in democracy while regarding popular participation in the exercise of power as "absurd and immoral." We lacked—and needed—sufficient courage to discuss with the common man his right to that participation. Nothing threatened the correct development of popular emergence more than an educational practice which failed to offer opportunities for the analysis and debate of problems, or for genuine participation; one which not only did not identify with the trend toward democratization but reinforced our lack of democratic experience.

We needed, then, an education which would lead men to take a new stance toward their problems—that of intimacy with those problems, one oriented toward research instead of repeating irrelevant principles. An education of "I wonder," instead of merely, "I do." Vitality, instead of insistence on the transmission of what Alfred North Whitehead has called "inert ideas—that is to say, ideas that are merely received into the mind without being utilised, or tested, or thrown into fresh combinations."[7]

---

7. *The Aims of Education and Other Essays* (New York, 1967), pp. 1–2.

Critics of the Brazilian taste for verbosity have customarily accused our education of being "theoretical," mistakenly equating theory with verbalism. On the contrary, we lacked theory—a theory of intervention in reality, the analytical contact with existence which enables one to substantiate and to experience that existence fully and completely. In this sense, theorizing is contemplation (although not in the erroneous connotation of abstraction or opposition to reality). Our education was *not* theoretical, precisely because it lacked this bent toward substantiation, toward invention, toward research.

Our traditional curriculum, disconnected from life, centered on words emptied of the reality they are meant to represent,[8] lacking in concrete activity, could never develop a critical consciousness. Indeed, its own naïve dependence on high-sounding phrases, reliance on rote, and tendency toward abstractness actually intensified our naïveté.[9]

Our verbal culture[10] corresponds to our inadequacy of dialogue, investigation, and research. As a matter of fact, I am increasingly convinced that the roots of the Brazilian taste for speeches, for "easy" words, for a well-turned phrase, lie in our lack of democratic experience. The fewer the democratic experiences which lead through concrete participation in reality to critical consciousness of it, the more a group tends to perceive and to confront that reality na-

8. In this regard, see the excellent observations of Fromm on the alienation of language. "...One must always be aware of the danger of the spoken word, that it threatens to substitute itself for the living experience." *Marx's Concept of Man*, Erich Fromm, ed. (New York, 1957), p. 45.
9. Two generations of Brazilian educators, joined by sociologists concerned with education, have insisted on this point, and on the necessity for a new educational perspective increasingly directed toward development. Those who have published essays and articles on this topic in specialized journals (e.g., the *Revista Brasileira de Estudos Pedagógicos*) include Anísio Teixeira, Fernando de Azevedo, Lourenço Filho, Carneiro Leão, and others among the older generation; and Roberto Moreira, Arthur Rios, Lauro de Oliveira Lima, Paulo de Almeida Campos, Florestan Fernandes (primarily a sociologist), Guerreiro Ramos (a sociologist), and others among the younger men. Brazilian economists have also made lucid and important forays into this field. Notwithstanding these efforts, the major emphasis of Brazilian education has been that described in this essay.
10. See Fernando de Azevedo, *Brazilian Culture*, perhaps the best work on this topic published in Brazil.

ïvely, to represent it verbosely. The less critical capacity a group possesses, the more ingenuously it treats problems and the more superficially it discusses subjects.

It was the climate of transition which had finally led us to identify with our reality in a systematic way. I was concerned to take advantage of that climate to attempt to rid our education of its wordiness, its lack of faith in the student and his power to discuss, to work, to create. Democracy and democratic education are founded on faith in men, on the belief that they not only can but should discuss the problems of their country, of their continent, their world, their work, the problems of democracy itself. Education is an act of love, and thus an act of courage. It cannot fear the analysis of reality or, under pain of revealing itself as a farce, avoid creative discussion.

The Brazilian tradition, however, has not been to exchange ideas, but to dictate them; not to debate or discuss themes, but to give lectures; not to work *with* the student, but to work *on* him, imposing an order to which he has had to accommodate. By giving the student formulas to receive and store, we have not offered him the means for authentic thought; assimilation results from search, from the effort to re-create and re-invent.

The existing form of education simply could not prepare men for integration in the process of democratization, because it contradicted that very process and opposed the emergence of the people into Brazilian public life. And since our cultural history had not provided us even with habits of political and social solidarity appropriate to our democratic form of government, we had to appeal to education as a cultural action by means of which the Brazilian people could learn, in place of the old passivity, new attitudes and habits of participation and intervention.[11] We had also to accept

---

11. I am aware that education is not a miraculous process capable by itself of effecting the changes necessary to move a nation from one epoch to another. Indeed, it is true that by itself education can do nothing, because the very fact of being "by itself" (i.e., superimposed on its context) nullifies its undeniable power as an instrument of change. Thus one cannot view "edu-

the challenge of our alarming rates of illiteracy, and ideally, since a literacy program was only part of the need, to work on it and education for intervention simultaneously.

It was true that in some regions of the country universities had made a noteworthy effort to prepare technicians, professionals, researchers, and scientists. But while we could not afford to lose the battle for development, which urgently required an increase in technical personnel at all levels, neither could we afford to lose the battle for the humanization of the Brazilian people. It was essential to harmonize a truly humanist position with technology by an education which would not leave technicians naïve and uncritical in dealing with problems other than those of their own specialty.[12]

Along these lines, I wish to mention two experiments of the greatest importance in university and graduate instruction: the Instituto Superior de Estudos Brasileiros (ISEB) and the University of Brasília. Both efforts were frustrated by the military *coup* of 1964.

Until the formation of ISEB, the point of reference for the majority of Brazilian intellectuals was Brazil as an object of European or North American thought. As a rule, they thought about Brazil from a non-Brazilian point of view; our cultural development was judged according to criteria and perspectives in which Brazil itself constituted a foreign element. The Brazilian intellectual lived in an imag-

---

cation as an absolute value, nor the school as an unconditioned institution," in the words of Luiz de Aguiar Costa Pinto (*Sociologia e Desenvolvimento,* Rio de Janeiro, 1965). On this subject, see also Roberto Moreira, *Educação e Desenvolvimento no Brasil* (Rio de Janeiro, 1960), and "Hipóteses e Diretrizes para o Estudo das Resistências à Mudança Social, Tendo em Vista a Educação e a Instrução Pública como Condições ou Fatôres," *Revista da Associação Pedagógica de Curitiba* (Paraná, 1959).

12. As Jacques Maritain has pointed out, "If we remember that the animal is a specialist, and a perfect one, all of its knowing-power being fixed upon a single task to be done, we ought to conclude that an educational program which would only aim at forming specialists ever more perfect in ever more specialized fields, and unable to pass judgment on any matter that goes beyond their specialized competence, would lead indeed to a progressive animalization of the human mind and life." *Education at the Crossroads* (New Haven, 1943), p. 19.

inary world, which he could not transform. Turning his back on his own world, sick of it, he suffered because Brazil was not Europe or the United States. Because he adopted the European view of Brazil as a backward country, he negated Brazil; the more he wanted to be a man of culture, the less he wanted to be a Brazilian. ISEB, which reflected the climate of dis-alienation characteristic of the transitional phase, constituted the negation of this negation by thinking of Brazil as its own reality, as a project. To think of Brazil as a Subject was to identify oneself with Brazil as it really was. The power of the ISEB thinking had its origins in this integration with the newly discovered and newly valued national reality. Two important consequences emerged: the creative power of intellectuals who placed themselves at the service of the national culture, and commitment to the destiny of the reality those intellectuals considered and assumed as their own. It was not by accident that ISEB, although it was not a university, spoke to and was heard by an entire university generation and, although it was not a workers' organization, gave conferences in trade unions.

Thinking of Brazil as a Subject also characterized the University of Brasília, which deliberately avoided the importation of alienated models. It did not seek to graduate verbose generalists, nor to prepare "technicistic" specialists, but rather to help transform the Brazilian reality, on the basis of a true understanding of its process.

The influence of these two institutions can be understood in terms of their identification with the awakening of the national consciousness, advancing in search of the transformation of Brazil. In this sense, the message and the task of both continue.

Education and
Conscientização

My concern for the democratization of culture, within the context of fundamental democratization, required special attention to the quantitative and qualitative deficits in our education. In 1964, approximately four million school-age children lacked schools; there were sixteen million illiterates of fourteen years and older. These truly alarming deficits constituted obstacles to the development of the country and to the creation of a democratic mentality.

For more than fifteen years I had been accumulating experiences in the field of adult education, in urban and rural proletarian and subproletarian areas. Urban dwellers showed a surprising interest in education, associated directly to the transitivity of their consciousness; the inverse was true in rural areas. (Today, in some areas, that situation is already changing.) I had experimented with—and abandoned—various methods and processes of communication. Never, however, had I abandoned the conviction that only by working with the people could I achieve anything authentic on their behalf. Never had I believed that the democratization of culture meant either its vulgarization or simply passing on to the people prescriptions formulated in the teacher's office. I agreed with Mannheim that "as democratic processes become widespread, it becomes more and more difficult to permit the masses to remain in a state of ignorance."[1] Mannheim would not restrict his definition of ignorance to illiteracy, but would include the masses' lack of experience at participating and intervening in the historical process.

Experiences as the Coordinator of the Adult Education Project of the Movement of Popular Culture in Recife led to the maturing of my early educational convictions.

---

1. Karl Mannheim, *Freedom, Power, and Democratic Planning* (New York, 1950).

Through this project, we launched a new institution of popular culture, a "culture circle," since among us a school was a traditionally passive concept. Instead of a teacher, we had a coordinator; instead of lectures, dialogue; instead of pupils, group participants; instead of alienating syllabi, compact programs that were "broken down" and "codified" into learning units.

In the culture circles, we attempted through group debate either to clarify situations or to seek action arising from that clarification. The topics for these debates were offered us by the groups themselves. Nationalism, profit remittances abroad, the political evolution of Brazil, development, illiteracy, the vote for illiterates, democracy, were some of the themes which were repeated from group to group. These subjects and others were schematized as far as possible and presented to the groups with visual aids, in the form of dialogue. We were amazed by the results.

After six months of experience with the culture circles, we asked ourselves if it would not be possible to do something in the field of adult literacy which would give us similar results to those we were achieving in the analysis of aspects of Brazilian reality. We started with some data and added more, aided by the Service of Cultural Extension of the University of Recife, which I directed at the time and under whose auspices the experiment was conducted.

The first literacy attempt took place in Recife, with a group of five illiterates, of which two dropped out on the second or third day. The participants, who had migrated from rural areas, revealed a certain fatalism and apathy in regard to their problems. They were totally illiterate. At the twentieth meeting, we gave progress tests. To achieve greater flexibility, we used an epidiascope. We projected a slide on which two kitchen containers appeared. "Sugar" was written on one, "poison" on the other. And underneath, the caption: "Which of the two would you use in your orangeade?" We asked the group to try to read the question and to give the answer orally. They answered, laughing, after several seconds, "Sugar." We followed the same procedure with other tests, such as recognizing bus lines and public buildings. During the twenty-first hour of study, one of the participants wrote, confidently, "I am amazed at myself."

From the beginning, we rejected the hypothesis of a purely mechanistic literacy program and considered the problem of teaching adults how to read in relation to the awakening of their consciousness. We wished to design a project in which we would attempt to move from naïveté to a critical attitude at the same time we taught reading. We wanted a literacy program which would be an introduction to the democratization of culture, a program with men as its Subjects rather than as patient recipients,[2] a program which itself would be an act of creation, capable of releasing other creative acts, one in which students would develop the impatience and vivacity which characterize search and invention.

We began with the conviction that the role of man was not only to be in the world, but to engage in relations with the world—that through acts of creation and re-creation, man makes cultural reality and thereby adds to the natural world, which he did not make. We were certain that man's relation to reality, expressed as a Subject to an object, results in knowledge, which man could express through language.

This relation, as is already clear, is carried out by men whether or not they are literate. It is sufficient to be a person to perceive the data of reality, to be capable of knowing, even if this knowledge is mere opinion. There is no such thing as absolute ignorance or absolute wisdom.[3] But men do not perceive those data in a pure form. As they appre-

---

2. In most reading programs, the students must endure an abysm between their own experience and the contents offered for them to learn. It requires patience indeed, after the hardships of a day's work (or of a day without work), to tolerate lessons dealing with "wing." "Johnny saw the wing." "The wing is on the bird." Lessons talking of Graces and grapes to men who never knew a Grace and never ate a grape. "Grace saw the grape."

3. No one ignores everything, just as no one knows everything. The dominating consciousness absolutizes ignorance in order to manipulate the so-called "uncultured." If some men are "totally ignorant," they will be incapable of managing themselves, and will need the orientation, the "direction," the "leadership" of those who consider themselves to be "cultured" and "superior."

hend a phenomenon or a problem, they also apprehend its causal links. The more accurately men grasp true causality, the more critical their understanding of reality will be. Their understanding will be magical to the degree that they fail to grasp causality. Further, critical consciouness always submits that causality to analysis; what is true today may not be so tomorrow. Naïve consciousness sees causality as a static, established fact, and thus is deceived in its perception.

Critical consciousness represents "things and facts as they exist empirically, in their causal and circumstantial correlations ... naïve consciousness considers itself superior to facts, in control of facts, and thus free to understand them as it pleases."[4]

Magic consciousness, in contrast, simply apprehends facts and attributes to them a superior power by which it is controlled and to which it must therefore submit. Magic consciousness is characterized by fatalism, which leads men to fold their arms, resigned to the impossibility of resisting the power of facts.

Critical consciousness is integrated with reality; naïve consciousness superimposes itself on reality; and fanatical consciousness, whose pathological naïveté leads to the irrational, adapts to reality.

It so happens that to every understanding, sooner or later an action corresponds. Once man perceives a challenge, understands it, and recognizes the possibilities of response, he acts. The nature of that action corresponds to the nature of his understanding. Critical understanding leads to critical action; magic understanding to magic response.

We wanted to offer the people the means by which they could supersede their magic or naïve perception of reality by one that was predominantly critical, so that they could assume positions appropriate to the dynamic climate of the transition. This meant that we must take the people at the point of emergence and, by helping them move from naïve

---

4. Álvaro Vieira Pinto, *Consciência e Realidade Nacional* (Rio de Janeiro, 1961).

to critical transitivity, facilitate their intervention in the historical process.

But how could this be done?

The answer seemed to lie:

a) in an active, *dialogical,* critical and criticism-stimulating *method;*

b) in changing the *program content* of education;

c) in the use of *techniques* like thematic "breakdown" and "codification"[5]

Our method, then, was to be based on dialogue, which is a horizontal relationship between persons.

DIALOGUE

A with B = communication
intercommunication

Relation of "empathy" between two "poles" who are engaged in a joint search.

MATRIX: Loving, humble, hopeful, trusting, critical.

Born of a critical matrix, dialogue creates a critical attitude (Jaspers). It is nourished by love, humility, hope, faith, and trust. When the two "poles" of the dialogue are thus linked by love, hope, and mutual trust, they can join in a critical search for something. Only dialogue truly communicates.

Dialogue is the only way, not only in the vital questions of the political order, but in all the expressions of our being. Only by virtue of faith, however, does dialogue have power and meaning: by faith in man and his possibilities, by the faith that I can only become truly myself when other men also become themselves.[6]

And so we set dialogue in opposition with the anti-dialogue which was so much a part of our historical-cultural

---

5. "Breakdown": a splitting of themes into their fundamental nuclei. See *Pedagogy of the Oppressed*, p. 113ff. "Codification": the representation of a theme in the form of an existential situation. See *Pedagogy*, pp. 106–107 and pp. 114–115. (Translator's Note.)
6. Karl Jaspers, *op. cit.*

formation, and so present in the climate of transition.

ANTI-DIALOGUE

A
$\bigg/\!\!\bigg|$ over

B = communiqué

Relation of "empathy" is broken.

MATRIX: Loveless, arrogant, hopeless, mistrustful, acritical.

It involves vertical relationships between persons. It lacks love, is therefore acritical, and cannot create a critical attitude. It is self-sufficient and hopelessly arrogant. In antidialogue the relation of empathy between the "poles" is broken. Thus, anti-dialogue does not communicate, but rather issues communiqués.[7]

Whoever enters into dialogue does so with someone about something; and that something ought to constitute the new content of our proposed education. We felt that even before teaching the illiterate to read, we could help him to overcome his magic or naïve understanding and to develop an increasingly critical understanding. Toward this end, the first dimension of our new program content would be the anthropological concept of culture—that is, the distinction between the world of nature and the world of culture; the active role of men *in* and *with* their reality; the role of mediation which nature plays in relationships and communication among men; culture as the addition made by men to a world they did not make; culture as the result of men's labor, of their efforts to create and re-create; the transcendental meaning of human relationships; the humanist dimension of culture; culture as a systematic acquisition of human experience (but as creative assimilation, not as information-storing); the democratization of culture; the learning of reading and writing as a key to the world of written communication. In short, the role of man as Subject in the world and with the world.

---

7. See Jaspers, *op. cit.*

From that point of departure, the illiterate would begin to effect a change in his former attitudes, by discovering himself to be a maker of the world of culture, by discovering that he, as well as the literate person, has a creative and re-creative impulse. He would discover that culture is just as much a clay doll made by artists who are his peers as it is the work of a great sculptor, a great painter, a great mystic, or a great philosopher; that culture is the poetry of lettered poets and also the poetry of his own popular songs—that culture is all human creation.

To introduce the concept of culture, first we "broke down" this concept into its fundamental aspects. Then, on the basis of this breakdown, we "codified" (i.e., represented visually) ten existential situations. These situations are presented in the Appendix, together with a brief description of some of the basic elements contained in each. Each representation contained a number of elements to be "decoded" by the group participants, with the help of the coordinator. Francisco Brenand, one of the greatest contemporary Brazilian artists, painted these codifications, perfectly integrating education and art.

It is remarkable to see with what enthusiasm these illiterates engage in debate and with what curiosity they respond to questions implicit in the codifications. In the words of Odilon Ribeiro Coutinho, these "detemporalized men begin to integrate themselves in time." As the dialogue intensifies, a "current" is established among the participants, dynamic to the degree that the content of the codifications corresponds to the existential reality of the groups.

Many participants during these debates affirm happily and self-confidently that they are not being shown "anything new, just remembering." "I make shoes," said one, "and now I see that I am worth as much as the Ph.D. who writes books."

"Tomorrow," said a street-sweeper in Brasília, "I'm going to go to work with my head high." He had discovered the value of his person. "I know now that I am cultured," an elderly peasant said emphatically. And when he was asked how it was that now he knew himself to be cultured, he answered with the same emphasis, "Because I work, and working, I transform the world."[8]

Once the group has perceived the distinction between the two worlds—nature and culture—and recognized man's role in each, the coordinator presents situations focusing on or expanding other aspects of culture.

The participants go on to discuss culture as a systematic acquisition of human experience, and to discover that in a lettered culture this acquisition is not limited to oral transmission, as is the case in unlettered cultures which lack graphic signs. They conclude by debating the democratization of culture, which opens the perspective of acquiring literacy.

All these discussions are critical, stimulating, and highly motivating. The illiterate perceives critically that it is necessary to learn to read and write, and prepares himself to become the agent of this learning.

To acquire literacy is more than to psychologically and mechanically dominate reading and writing techniques. It is to dominate these techniques in terms of consciousness; to understand what one reads and to write what one understands; it is to *communicate* graphically. Acquiring literacy does not involve memorizing sentences, words, or syllables —lifeless objects unconnected to an existential universe— but rather an attitude of creation and re-creation, a self-transformation producing a stance of intervention in one's context.

Thus the educator's role is fundamentally to enter into dialogue with the illiterate about concrete situations and simply to offer him the instruments with which he can teach himself to read and write. This teaching cannot be done from the top down, but only from the inside out, by the illiterate himself, with the collaboration of the educator. That is why we searched for a method which would be the instrument of the learner as well as of the educator, and which, in the lucid observation of a young Brazilian sociolo-

---

8. Similar responses were evoked by the programs carried out in Chile.

gist,[9] "would identify learning *content* with the learning *process*."

Hence, our mistrust in primers,[10] which set up a certain grouping of graphic signs as a gift and cast the illiterate in the role of the *object* rather than the *Subject* of his learning. Primers, even when they try to avoid this pitfall, end by *donating* to the illiterate words and sentences which really should result from his own creative effort. We opted instead for the use of "generative words," those whose syllabic elements offer, through re-combination, the creation of new words. Teaching men how to read and write a syllabic language like Portuguese means showing them how to grasp critically the way its words are formed, so that they themselves can carry out the creative play of combinations. Fifteen or eighteen words seemed sufficient to present the basic phonemes of the Portuguese language. The seventeen generative words used in the State of Rio are presented in the Appendix.

The program is elaborated in several phases:

Phase 1 Researching the vocabulary of the groups with which one is working. This research is carried out during informal encounters with the inhabitants of the area. One selects not only the words most weighted with existential meaning (and thus the greatest emotional content), but also typical sayings, as well as words and expressions linked to the experience of the groups in which the researcher participates. These interviews reveal longings, frustrations, disbeliefs, hopes, and an impetus to participate. During this initial phase the team of educators form rewarding relationships and discover often unsuspected exuberance and beauty in the people's language.

The archives of the Service of Cultural Extension of the University of Recife contain vocabulary studies of rural and

---

9. Celso Beisegel, in an unpublished work.
10. I am not opposed to reading texts, which are in fact indispensable to developing the visual-graphic channel of communication and which in great part should be elaborated by the participants themselves. I should add that our experience is based on the use of multiple channels of communication.

urban areas in the Northeast and in southern Brazil full of such examples as the following:

"The month of January in Angicos," said a man from the backlands of Rio Grande do Norte, "is a hard one to live through, because January is a tough guy who makes us suffer." (*Janeiro em Angicos é duro de se viver, porque janeiro é cabra danado para judiar de nós.*)

"I want to learn to read and write," said an illiterate from Recife, "so that I can stop being the shadow of other people."

A man from Florianópolis: "The people have an answer."

Another, in an injured tone: "I am not angry (*não tenho paixão*) at being poor, but at not knowing how to read."

"I have the school of the world," said an illiterate from the southern part of the country, which led Professor Jomard de Brito to ask in an essay, "What can one presume to 'teach' an adult who affirms 'I have the school of the world'?"[11]

"I want to learn to read and to write so I can change the world," said an illiterate from São Paulo, for whom *to know* quite correctly meant *to intervene* in his reality.

"The people put a screw in their heads," said another in somewhat esoteric language. And when he was asked what he meant, he replied in terms revealing the phenomenon of popular emergence: "That is what explains that you, Professor, have come to talk with me, the people."

Such affirmations merit interpretation by specialists, to produce a more efficient instrument for the educator's action.[12] The generative words to be used in the program should emerge from this field vocabulary research, not from the educator's personal inspiration, no matter how proficiently he might construct a list.

Phase 2 Selection of the generative words from the vo-

---

11. "Educação de Adultos e Unificação de Cultura," Estudos Universitários, *Revista de Cultura*, Universidade de Recife, 2–4, 1963.
12. Luís Costa Lima, Professor of Literary Theory, has analyzed many of these texts by illiterate authors.

cabulary which was studied. The following criteria should govern their selection:

a) phonemic richness;

b) phonetic difficulty (the words chosen should correspond to the phonetic difficulties of the language, placed in a sequence moving gradually from words of less to those of greater difficulty);

c) pragmatic tone, which implies a greater engagement of a word in a given social, cultural and political reality

Professor Jarbas Maciel has commented that "these criteria are contained in the semeiotic criterion: the best generative word is that which combines the greatest possible 'percentage' of the syntactic criteria (phonemic richness, degree of complex phonetic difficulty, 'manipulability' of the groups of signs, the syllables, etc.), the semantic criteria (greater or lesser 'intensity' of the link between the word and the thing it designates), the greater or lesser correspondence between the word and the pragmatic thing designated, the greater or lesser quality of *conscientização* which the word potentially carries, or the grouping of sociocultural reactions which the word generates in the person or group using it."[13]

Phase 3 The creation of the "codifications:" the representation of typical existential situations of the group with which one is working. These representations function as challenges, as coded situation-problems containing elements to be decoded by the groups with the collaboration of the coordinator. Discussion of these codifications will lead the groups toward a more critical consciousness at the same time that they begin to learn to read and write. The codifications represent familiar local situations—which, however, open perspectives for the analysis of regional and national problems. The generative words are set into the codifications, graduated according to their phonetic difficulty. One

---

13. "A Fundamentação Teórica do Sistema Paulo Freire de Educação," *Estudos Universitários, Revista de Cultura,* Universidade do Recife, No. IV, 1963.

generative word may embody the entire situation, or it may refer to only one of the elements of the situation.

Phase 4 The elaboration of agendas, which should serve as mere aids to the coordinators, never as rigid schedules to be obeyed.

Phase 5 The preparation of cards with the breakdown of the phonemic families which correspond to the generative words.[14]

A major problem in setting up the program is instructing the teams of coordinators. Teaching the purely technical aspect of the procedure is not difficult; the difficulty lies rather in the creation of a new attitude—that of dialogue, so absent in our own upbringing and education. The coordinators must be converted to dialogue in order to carry out education rather than domestication. Dialogue is an I-Thou relationship, and thus necessarily a relationship between two Subjects. Each time the "thou" is changed into an object, an "it," dialogue is subverted and education is changed to deformation. The period of instruction must be followed by dialogical supervision, to avoid the temptation of anti-dialogue on the part of the coordinators.

Once the material has been prepared in the form of slides, filmstrips, or posters, once the teams of coordinators and supervisors have been instructed in all aspects of the method and have been given their agendas, the program itself can begin. It functions in the following manner:

The codified situation is projected, together with the first generative word, which graphically represents the oral expression of the object perceived. Debate about its implications follows.

Only after the group, with the collaboration of the coordinator, has exhausted the analysis (decoding) of the situation, does the coordinator call attention to the generative word, encouraging the participants to visualize (not memorize) it. Once the word has been visualized, and the semantic link established between the word and the object to

---

14. See p. 82 of the Appendix.

which it refers, the word is presented alone on another slide (or poster or photogram) without the object it names. Then the same word is separated into syllables, which the illiterate usually identifies as "pieces." Once the "pieces" are recognized, the coordinator presents visually the phonemic families which compose the word, first in isolation and then together, to arrive at the recognition of the vowels. The card presenting the phonemic families has been called the "discovery card."[15] Using this card to reach a synthesis, men discover the mechanism of word formation through phonemic combinations in a syllabic language like Portuguese. By appropriating this mechanism critically (not learning it by rote), they themselves can begin to produce a system of graphic signs. They can begin, with surprising ease, to create words with the phonemic combinations offered by the breakdown of a trisyllabic word, on the first day of the program.[16]

For example, let us take the word *tijolo* (brick) as the first generative word, placed in a "situation" of construction work. After discussing the situation in all its possible aspects, the semantic link between the word and the object it names is established. Once the word has been noted within the situation, it is presented without the object: *tijolo*.

Afterwards: *ti-jo-lo*. By moving immediately to present the "pieces" visually, we initiate the recognition of phonemic families. Beginning with the first syllable, *ti*, the group is motivated to learn the whole phonemic family resulting

---

15. Aurenice Cardoso, "Conscientização e Alfabetização—Visão Prática do Sistema Paulo Freire de Educação de Adultos," Estudos Universitários, *Revista de Cultura*, Universidade do Recife, No. II, 1963.
16. Generally, in a period of six weeks to two months, we could leave a group of twenty-five persons reading newspapers, writing notes and simple letters, and discussing problems of local and national interest.
Each culture circle was equipped with a Polish-made projector, imported at the cost of about $13.00. Since we had not yet set up our own laboratory, a filmstrip cost us about $7–$8. We also used an inexpensive blackboard. The slides were projected on the wall of the house where the culture circle met or, where this was difficult, on the reverse side (painted white) of the blackboard.
The Education Ministry imported 35,000 of the projectors, which after the military coup of 1964 were presented on television as "highly subversive."

from the combination of the initial consonant with the other vowels. The group then learns the second family through the visual presentation of *jo,* and finally arrives at the third family.

When the phonemic family is projected, the group at first recognizes only the syllable of the word which has been shown:

(ta-te-*ti*-to-tu), (ja-je-ji-*jo*-ju), (la-le-li-*lo*-lu)

When the participants recognize *ti,* from the generative word *tijolo,* it is proposed that they compare it with the other syllables; whereupon they discover that while all the syllables begin the same, they end differently. Thus, they cannot all be called *ti.*

The same procedure is followed with the syllables *jo* and *lo* and their families. After learning each phonemic family, the group practices reading the new syllables.

The most important moment arises when the three families are presented together:

ta-te-ti-to-tu
ja-je-ji-jo-ju   THE DISCOVERY CARD
la-le-li-lo-lu

After one horizontal and one vertical reading to grasp the vocal sounds, the group (*not* the coordinator) begins to carry out oral synthesis. One by one, they all begin to "make" words with the combinations available:[17]

tatu (armadillo), *luta* (struggle), *lajota* (small flagstone), *loja* (store), *jato* (jet), *juta* (jute), *lote* (lot), *lula* (squid), *tela* (screen), etc. There are even some participants who take a vowel from one of the syllables, link it to another syllable, and add a third, thus forming a word. For example, they take the *i* from li, join it to *le* and add *te: leite* (milk).

There are others, like an illiterate from Brasília, who on the first night he began his literacy program said, "*tu já lê*" ("you already read").[18]

---

17. In a television interview, Gilson Amado observed lucidly, "They can do this, because there is no such thing as oral illiteracy."
18. In correct Portuguese, *tu já lês.*

The oral exercises involve not only learning, but recognition (without which there is no true learning). Once these are completed, the participants begin—on that same first evening—to write. On the following day they bring from home as many words as they were able to make with the combinations of the phonemes they learned. It doesn't matter if they bring combinations which are not actual words—what does matter is the discovery of the mechanism of phonemic combinations.

The group itself, with the help of the educator (*not* the educator with the help of the group), should test the words thus created. A group in the state of Rio Grande do Norte called those combinations which were actual words "thinking words" and those which were not, "dead words".

Not infrequently, after assimilating the phonemic mechanism by using the "discovery card," participants would write words with complex phonemes (*tra, nha,* etc.), which had not yet been presented to them. In one of the Culture Circles in Angicos, Rio Grande do Norte, on the fifth day of discussion, in which simple phonemes were being shown, one of the participants went to the blackboard to write (as he said) "a thinking word." He wrote: "*o povo vai resouver os poblemas do Brasil votando conciente*"[19] ("the people will solve the problems of Brazil by informed voting"). In such cases, the group discussed the text, debating its significance in the context of their reality.

How can one explain the fact that a man who was illiterate several days earlier could write words with complex phonemes before he had even studied them? Once he had dominated the mechanism of phonemic combinations, he attempted—and managed—to express himself graphically, in the way he spoke.[20]

---

19. *resouver* is a corruption of *resolver;* *poblemas* a corruption of *problemas;* the letter *s* is lacking from the syllable *cons.*

20. Interestingly enough, as a rule the illiterates wrote confidently and legibly, largely overcoming the natural indecisiveness of beginners. Elza Freire thinks this may be due to the fact that these persons, beginning with the discussion of the anthropological concept of culture, discovered themselves to be more fully human, thereby acquiring an increasing emotional confidence in their learning which was reflected in their motor activity.

I wish to emphasize that in educating adults, to avoid a rote, mechanical process one must make it possible for them to achieve critical consciousness so that they can teach themselves to read and write.

As an active educational method helps a person to become consciously aware of his context and his condition as a human being as Subject, it will become an instrument of choice. At that point he will become politicized. When an ex-illiterate of Angicos, speaking before President João Goulart and the presidential staff,[21] declared that he was no longer part of the *mass,* but one of the *people,* he had done more than utter a mere phrase; he had made a conscious option. He had chosen decisional participation, which belongs to the people, and had renounced the emotional resignation of the masses. He had become political.

The National Literacy Program of the Ministry of Education and Culture, which I coordinated, planned to extend and strengthen this education work throughout Brazil. Obviously we could not confine that work to a literacy program, even one which was critical rather than mechanical. With the same spirit of a pedagogy of communication, we were therefore planning a post-literacy stage which would vary only as to curriculum. If the National Literacy Program had not been terminated by the military coup, in 1964 there would have been more than 20,000 culture circles functioning throughout the country. In these, we planned to investigate the themes of the Brazilian people. These themes would be analyzed by specialists and broken down into learning units, as we had done with the concept of culture and with the coded situations linked to the generative words. We would prepare filmstrips with these breakdowns as well as simplified texts with references to the original texts. By gathering this thematic material, we could have offered a substantial post-literacy program. Further, by making a catalog of thematic breakdowns and bibliographic references

---

21. I wish to acknowledge the support given our efforts by President Goulart, by Ministers of Education Paulo de Tarso and Júlio Sambaquy, and by the Rector of the University of Recife, Professor João Alfredo da Costa Lima.

available to high schools and colleges, we could widen the sphere of the program and help identify our schools with our reality.

At the same time, we began to prepare material with which we could carry out concretely an education that would encourage what Aldous Huxley has called the "art of dissociating ideas"[22] as an antidote to the domesticating power of propaganda.[23] We planned filmstrips, for use in the literacy phase, presenting propaganda—from advertising commercials to ideological indoctrination—as a "problem-situation" for discussion.

For example, as men through discussion begin to perceive the deceit in a cigarette advertisement featuring a beautiful, smiling woman in a bikini (i.e., the fact that she, her smile, her beauty, and her bikini have nothing at all to do with the cigarette), they begin to discover the difference between education and propaganda. At the same time, they are preparing themselves to discuss and perceive the same deceit in ideological or political propaganda;[24] they are arming them-

---

22. *Ends and Means* (New York and London, 1937), p. 252.
23. I have never forgotten the publicity (done cleverly, considering our acritical mental habits) for a certain Brazilian public figure. The bust of the candidate was displayed with arrows pointing to his head, his eyes, his mouth, and his hands. Next to the arrows appeared the legend:

> You don't need to think, he thinks for you!
> You don't need to see, he sees for you!
> You don't need to talk, he talks for you!
> You don't need to act, he acts for you!

24. In the campaigns carried out against me, I have been called "ignorant" and "illiterate," "the author of a method so innocuous that it did not even manage to teach him how to read and write." It was said that I was not "the inventor" of dialogue (as if I had ever made such an irresponsible affirmation). It was said that I had done "nothing original," and that I had "plagiarized European or North-American educators," as well as the author of a Brazilian primer. (On the subject of originality, I have always agreed with Dewey, for whom originality does not lie in the "extraordinary and fanciful," but "in putting everyday things to uses which had not occurred to others." *Democracy and Education*, New York, 1916, p. 187.)
None of these accusations has ever wounded me. What does leave me perplexed is to hear or read that I intended to "Bolchevize the country" with my method. In fact, my actual crime was that I treated literacy as more than a mechanical problem, and linked it to *conscientização*, which was "dangerous." It was that I viewed education as an effort to liberate men, not as yet another instrument to dominate them.

selves to "dissociate ideas." In fact, this has always seemed to me to be the way to defend democracy, not a way to subvert it.

One subverts democracy (even though one does this in the name of democracy) by making it irrational; by making it rigid in order "to defend it against totalitarian rigidity"; by making it hateful, when it can only develop in a context of love and respect for persons; by closing it, when it only lives in openness; by nourishing it with fear when it must be courageous; by making it an instrument of the powerful in the oppression of the weak; by militarizing it against the people; by alienating a nation in the name of democracy.

One defends democracy by leading it to the state Mannheim calls "militant democracy"—a democracy which does not fear the people, which suppresses privilege, which can plan without becoming rigid, which defends itself without hate, which is nourished by a critical spirit rather than irrationality.

Postscript

Today, the task of overcoming our lack of democratic experience through experiences in participation still awaits us, as does the task of superseding the irrational climate which prevails in Brazil.

It is too soon to say to what extent this climate can be overcome without provoking larger explosions and even more severe forms of retreat. Possibly the intense emotionality generated by irrational sectarianism can open a new way within the historical process which will lead less rapidly to more authentic and human forms of life for the Brazilian people.

Appendix

The following drawings represent the "situations" discussed in the culture circles. The originals, by Francisco Brenand, were taken from me; these were done by another Brazilian artist, Vicente de Abreu, now in exile.

FIRST SITUATION

Man in the World and with The World, Nature and Culture

Through the discussion of this situation—man as a being of relationships—the participants arrive at the distinction between two worlds: that of nature and that of culture. They perceive the normal situation of man as a being in the world and with the world, as a creative and re-creative being who, through work, constantly alters reality. By means of simple questions, such as, "Who made the well? Why did he do it? How did he do it? When?" which are repeated with regard to the other "elements" of the situation, two basic concepts emerge: that of *necessity* and that of *work;* and culture becomes explicit on a primary level, that of subsistence. The man made the well because he needed water. And he did it because, relating to the world, he made the latter the object of his knowledge. By work, he submitted the world to a process of transformation. Thus, he made the house, his clothes, his work tools. From that point, one discusses with the group, in obviously simple but critically objective terms, the relations among men, which unlike those discussed previously cannot be either of domination or transformation, because they are relations among Subjects.

SECOND SITUATION

DIALOGUE MEDIATED BY NATURE

In the first situation, we reached the analysis of relationships among men, which, because they are relations among Subjects, cannot be those of domination. Now, confronted by this second situation, the group is motivated to analyze dialogue, interpersonal communication, the encounter of consciousnesses; motivated to analyze the mediation of the world—as transformed and humanized by men—in this communication; motivated to analyze the loving, humble, hopeful, critical, and creative foundation of dialogue.

The three situations which follow constitute a series, the analysis of which validates the concept of culture at the same time in which other aspects of real interest are discussed.

THIRD SITUATION

Unlettered Hunter

The debate is initiated by distinguishing in this situation what belongs to nature and what belongs to culture. "Culture in this picture," the participants say, "is the bow, it is the arrow, it is the feathers the Indian wears." And when they are asked if the feathers are not nature, they always answer, "The feathers are nature, while they are on the bird. After man kills the bird, takes the feathers, and transforms them with work, they are not nature any longer. They are culture." (I had the opportunity to hear this reply innumerable times, in various regions of the country.) By distinguishing the historical-cultural period of the hunter from their own, the participants arrive at the perception of what constitutes an unlettered culture. They discover that when man prolongs his arms five to ten yards by making an implement and therefore no longer needs to catch his prey with his hands, he has created culture. By transferring not only the use of the implement, but the incipient technology of its manufacture, to younger generations, he has created education. The participants discuss how education occurs in an unlettered culture, where one cannot properly speak of illiterates. They then perceive immediately that to be illiterate is to belong to an unlettered culture and to fail to dominate the techniques of reading and writing. For some, this perception is dramatic.

FOURTH SITUATION

Lettered Hunter (Lettered Culture)

When this situation is projected, the participants identify
the hunter as a man of their culture, although he may be
illiterate. They discuss the technological advance represented by the rifle as compared with the bow and arrow.
They analyze man's increasing opportunity, because of his
work and his creative spirit, to transform the world. They
discuss the fact that this transformation, however, has
meaning only to the extent that it contributes to the humanization of man, and is employed toward his liberation. They
finally analyze the implications of education for development.

FIFTH SITUATION

THE HUNTER AND THE CAT

With this situation, the participants discuss the fundamental aspects which characterize the different forms of being in the world—those of men and of animals. They discuss man as a being who not only knows, but knows that he knows; as a conscious being (*corpo consciente*) in the world; as a consciousness which in the process of becoming an authentic person emerges reflective and intent upon the world.

In regard to the preceding series, I will never forget an illiterate from Brasília who affirmed, with absolute self-confidence, "Of these three, only two are hunters—the two men. They are hunters because they make culture before and after they hunt." (He failed only to say that they made culture while they hunted.) "The third, the cat, does not make culture, either before or after the 'hunt.' He is not a hunter, he is a pursuer." By making this subtle distinction between hunting and pursuing, this man grasped the fundamental point: the creation of culture.

The debate of these situations produced a wealth of observations about men and animals, about creative power, freedom, intelligence, instinct, education, and training.

SIXTH SITUATION

Man Transforms the Material of Nature by His Work

"What do we see here? What are the men doing?" the coordinator asks. "They are working with clay," all the participants answer. "They are changing the materials of nature with work," many answer.

After a series of analyses of work (Some participants even speak of the "pleasure of making beautiful things," as did one man from Brasília), the coordinator asks whether the work represented in the situation will result in an object of culture. They answer yes: "A vase." "A jug." "A pot," etc.

SEVENTH SITUATION

A Vase, the Product of
Man's Work Upon the Material of Nature

During a discussion of this situation in a Culture Circle of Recife, I was moved to hear a woman say with emotion, "I make culture. I know how to make that." Many participants, referring to the flowers in the vase, say, "As flowers, they are nature. As decoration, they are culture." The esthetic dimension of the product, which in a sense had been awakened from the beginning, is now reinforced. This aspect will be discussed fully in the following situation, when culture is analyzed on the level of spiritual necessity.

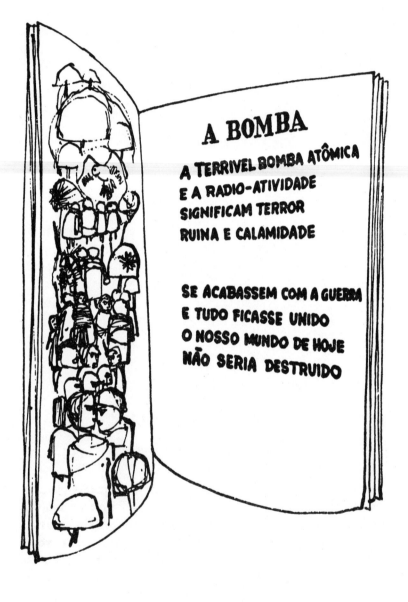

A BOMBA

A TERRIVEL BOMBA ATÔMICA
E A RADIO-ATIVIDADE
SIGNIFICAM TERROR
RUINA E CALAMIDADE

SE ACABASSEM COM A GUERRA
E TUDO FICASSE UNIDO
O NOSSO MUNDO DE HOJE
NÃO SERIA DESTRUIDO

EIGHTH SITUATION

POETRY

First the coordinator reads, slowly, the text which has been projected. "This is a poem," everyone usually says. The participants describe the poem as popular, saying that its author is a simple man of the people. They discuss whether or not the poem is culture. "It is culture, just as the vase is," they say, "but it is different from the vase." Through the discussion they perceive, in critical terms, that poetic expression, whose material is not the same, responds to a different necessity. After discussing aspects of popular and erudite artistic expression in various fields, the coordinator rereads the text and submits it to a group discussion.

"THE BOMB: The terrible atomic bomb / And radioactivity / Signify terror, / Ruin and calamity. / If war were ended, / And everything were united, / Our world / Would not be destroyed."

NINTH SITUATION

Patterns of Behavior

In this situation, we wish to analyze patterns of behavior as a cultural manifestation, in order subsequently to discuss resistance to change.

The picture presents a *gaucho* from the south of Brazil and a cowboy from the Brazilian northeast, each dressed in his customary fashion. Starting with the subject of their clothing, the discussion moves on to some of their forms of behavior. Once, in a Culture Circle in the south of Brazil, I heard the following: "We see here traditions of two Brazilian regions—the south and the northeast. Traditions of clothing. But before the traditions were formed, there was a need to dress like that—one with warm clothing, the other with thick leather clothing. Sometimes the need passes but the tradition goes on."

TENTH SITUATION

A CULTURE CIRCLE IN ACTION—
SYNTHESIS OF THE PREVIOUS DISCUSSIONS

On seeing this situation, the Culture Circle participants easily identify themselves. They discuss culture as a systematic acquisition of knowledge, and also the democratization of culture within the general context of fundamental democratization. "The democratization of culture," one of these anonymous illiterate teachers once said, "has to start from what we are and what we do as a people, not from what some people think and want for us." In addition to discussing culture and its democratization, the participants analyze the functioning of a Culture Circle, its dynamic significance, the creative power of dialogue and the clarification of consciousness.

The preceding situations are discussed in two sessions, strongly motivating the group to begin on the third night their literacy program, which they now see as a key to written communication.

Literacy makes sense only in these terms, as the consequence of men's beginning to reflect about their own capacity for reflection, about the world, about their position in the world, about their work, about their power to transform the world, about the encounter of consciousness—about literacy itself, which thereby ceases to be something external and becomes a part of them, comes as a creation from within them. I can see validity only in a literacy program in which men understand words in their true significance: as a force to transform the world. As illiterate men discover the relativity of ignorance and of wisdom, they destroy one of the myths by which false elites have manipulated them. Learning to read and write has meaning in that, by requiring men to reflect about themselves and about the world they are in and with, it makes them discover that the world is also theirs, that their work is not the price they pay for being men but rather a way of loving—and of helping the world to be a better place.

The following are the seventeen generative words selected from the "vocabular universe" gathered in the State of Rio de Janeiro and applicable also to Guanabara. I have not included the visual representations within which these words were presented, but have indicated some of the dimensions of reality which were analyzed in the discussion of those situations.

GENERATIVE WORDS

1) SLUM (*favela*)—fundamental necessities:
    Housing
    Food
    Clothing
    Health
    Education

I will repeat here, with the generative word *favela,* a breakdown similar to that of the word *tijolo* presented in Chapter 4. After analyzing the existential situation (a photograph showing a slum), in which the group discusses the problems of housing, food, clothing, health, and education in a slum and in which the group further perceives the slum as a problem situation, the coordinator proceeds to present visually the word *favela* with its semantic links.

a) First a slide appears showing only the word:
    FAVELA

b) Immediately afterward, another slide appears with the word separated into syllables:
    FA-VE-LA

c) Afterwards, the phonemic family:
    FA-FE-FI-FO-FU

d) On another slide:
    VA-VE-VI-VO-VU

e) Then:
    LA-LE-LI-LO-LU

f) Now, the three families together:
    FA-FE-FI-FO-FU
    VA-VE-VI-VO-VU   *Discovery card*
    LA-LE-LI-LO-LU

The group then begins to create words with the various combinations.

2) RAIN (*chuva*)

Aspects for discussion: The influence of the environment on human life.

The climatic factor in a subsistence economy.

Regional climatic imbalances in Brazil.

3) PLOW (*arado*)

Aspects for discussion: The value of human labor. Men and techniques: the process of transforming nature. Labor and capital. Agrarian reform.

4) LAND (*terreno*)

Aspects for discussion: Economic domination. The latifundium. Irrigation. Natural resources. Defense of the national patrimony.

5) FOOD (*comida*)

Aspects for discussion: Malnutrition. Hunger (from the local to the national sphere). Infant mortality and related diseases.

6) AFRO-BRAZILIAN DANCING (*batuque*)

Aspects for discussion: Popular culture. Folklore. Erudite culture. Cultural alienation.

7) WELL (*poço*)

Aspects for discussion: Health and endemic diseases. Sanitary education. Water supply.

8) BICYCLE (*bicicleta*)

Aspects for discussion: Transportation problems. Mass transportation.

9) WORK (*trabalho*)

Aspects for discussion: The process of transforming reality. Man's value through work. Manual, intellectual, and technological work. Craftsmanship. The dichotomy between manual and intellectual labor.

10) SALARY (*salário*)

Aspects for discussion: The economic sphere.

Man's situation

a) remuneration: salaried and non-salaried labor

b) the minimum wage

    c) *salário móvel* (adjustment of wages to changes in the cost of living)

11) PROFESSION (*profissão*)

Aspects for discussion: The social sphere. The problem of business. Social classes and social mobility. Trade unionism. Strikes.

12) GOVERNMENT (*govêrno*)

Aspects for discussion: The political sphere. Political power (the three powers). The role of the people in the organization of power. Popular participation.

13) SWAMPLANDS (*mangue*)

Aspects for discussion: The population of the swamplands. Paternalism. Assistencialism. Ascent by these populations from the position of object to that of Subject.

14) SUGAR MILL (*engenho*)

Aspects for discussion: The economic formation of Brazil. Monoculture. Latifundium. Agrarian reform.

15) HOE (*enxada*)

Aspects for discussion: Agrarian reform and banking reform. Technology and reforms.

16) BRICK (*tijolo*)

Aspects for discussion: Urban reform—fundamental aspects. Planning. The relationship between various reforms.

17) WEALTH (*riqueza*)

Aspects for discussion: Brazil and the universal dimension. The confrontation between wealth and poverty. Rich man vs. poor man. Rich nations vs. poor nations. Dominant nations and dominated nations. Developed and underdeveloped nations. National emancipation. Effective aid among nations and world peace.

Preface to "Extension or Communication" by Jacques Chonchol

Translated by Myra Bergman Ramos

Preface

In this essay, Paulo Freire, the internationally renowned Brazilian educator who recently lived and worked in Chile, analyzes how technicians and peasants can communicate in the process of developing a new agrarian society.

Freire's thought is profound and at times difficult to follow but penetrating; its essence reveals a new world of truths, relations among these truths, and a logical ordering of concepts. We perceive that words, their meaning, their context, the actions of men, their struggle to dominate the natural world and to create their culture and their history form a totality in which each aspect has significance not only in itself but in function of the whole.

More than just an analysis of the educational task of the agronomist (mistitled an "extension agent") the present essay seems to me to be a profound synthesis of the role Paulo Freire attributes to education understood in its true perspective: that of humanizing man through his conscious action to transform the world.

Freire begins his work by analyzing the term "extension" from different points of view: the linguistic meaning of the word, a criticism based on the philosophical theory of knowledge, and a study of the relations between the concepts of extension and cultural invasion. Subsequently he discusses agrarian reform and change, demonstrating the profound opposition which exists between extension and communication. The agronomist-educator, like teachers in general, must choose communication if he genuinely wants to reach men—not by being abstract, but by being concrete, within a historical reality.

Reading this essay makes us realize the poverty and limitations of the concept of agricultural extension which has prevailed among us and many other Latin-American countries, in spite of the generosity and good will of those who have dedicated their lives to this work. We can see how their failure to achieve more lasting results was due, in some cases, to their naïve view of reality, but more commonly to the marked attitude of superiority and domination with which the technician confronted the peasant within a traditional agrarian structure.

Freire shows us how the concept of extension leads to actions which transform the peasant into a "thing," an object of development projects which negate him as a being capable of transforming the world. In this concept the peasant is not educated but instead is treated as a depository for propaganda from an alien cultural world, containing the things which the technician (who is modern and therefore superior) thinks the peasant ought to know in order to become modern also.

Paulo Freire tells us, correctly, that:

Knowing, whatever its level, is not the act by which a subject transformed into an object docilely and passively accepts the contents others give or impose on him or her. Knowledge, on the contrary, necessitates the curious presence of subjects confronted with the world. It requires their transforming action on reality. It demands a constant searching. It implies invention and reinvention. . . . In the learning process the only person who really *learns* is s/he who appropriates what is learned, who apprehends and thereby reinvents that learning; s/he who is able to apply the appropriate learning to concrete existential situations. On the other hand, the person who is filled by another with "contents" whose meaning s/he is not aware of, which contradict his or her way of being in the world, cannot learn because s/he is not challenged.

In addition, Freire emphasizes that from a humanist and scientific perspective one cannot focus on technical capacitation except within the context of a total cultural reality. Peasant attitudes toward phenomena like planting, harvest, erosion, and reforesting are related to their attitudes toward nature, their religious beliefs, their values, and so forth. As a structure, this cultural totality cannot be affected in any of its parts without an automatic reflex occurring in the other dimensions. Thus, the agronomist-educator cannot bring about a change of peasant attitudes in regard to a particular aspect of life unless he knows their world view and confronts it in its totality.

I would like to stress the importance of Freire's criticism of the concept of extension as cultural invasion, as an attitude contrary to the dialogue which forms the basis of an authentic education. He likewise deals with the concept of domination, so frequently found at the heart of traditional education, and shows how the latter, instead of freeing men, enslaves them, reduces them to things, and manipulates them by not allowing them to act as Subjects in history and through this action to become authentic persons.

Also fundamental is Freire's analysis of the relationship between techniques, modernization and humanism, as he shows how to avoid the traditionalism of the status quo without falling into technological messianism. As he quite correctly affirms, while "all development is modernization, not all modernization is development."

I think this brief mention of themes is sufficient to emphasize the richness and depth of this essay which Paulo Freire has modestly titled *Extension or Communication*. I hope it will be widely read, considered, and debated, because I am certain it will make us more conscious of the reality in which we act, and thereby contribute to making us increasingly responsible and authentic.

JACQUES CHONCHOL

Santiago do Chile, April 1968

Extension or Communication

Translated by Louise Bigwood and Margaret Marshall

Chapter I

a) A SEMANTIC ANALYSIS OF THE TERM "EXTENSION"

A first concern in beginning this study is to make a critical analysis of the word extension. From a semantic stand-point words have a "basic meaning" and a "contextual meaning." It is the context in which a word is situated which determines its "potential" or "virtual" meanings, as Pierre Guiraud[1] terms them. For this reason, in each of the following contexts, the word extension has a specific meaning:

"This desk has an *extension* of three meters." "Color, in its essence, is the *extension* of the body." "The *extension* of the term *extension* was one of the subjects analyzed in the week of study." "The word 'structure,' which etymologically is basically connected with architecture, acquires a significant *extension* when it is used in economy, linguistics, psychology, anthropology, sociology, etc." "Pedro is an agronomist working in rural *extension*."[2] The meaning of extension in this last context constitutes the object of this investigation. The term extension, in the sense with which I am concerned here—that of the last context—implies the action of extending (more than in any of the cases cited) and of extending in its syntactical sense of a transitive relative verb with a double complement: to extend *something to*.

In this sense, the person who extends, extends something (direct object of the verbal action) to or towards someone (indirect object of the verbal action) who receives the content of the object of the verbal action. The expression "ex-

---

1. Guiraud, Pierre: *La Semántica, Fondo de Cultura,* Breviarios, 1965, p. 28.
2. Rural extension: designates the educational and technical assistance efforts of outside agencies acting through extension agents or extension workers to "extend" or transmit to peasants knowledge designed to improve farming practices, etc.

tension" in the context: "Pedro is an agronomist working in rural extension" means that Pedro is professionally engaged in an action which manifests itself in some kind of reality—an agricultural reality which would not exist as such if it were not for the existence of a human presence. His action, therefore, is that of the extension agent, who extends something towards someone. The rural extension agents would never think that their act of extending could have the meaning: "Charles extends his hands," although the same verb is used in the latter statement.

On the contrary, the role of extension agents is to extend, not their hands, but their knowledge and their technical capacities. For example, in an area designated for agricultural improvement as it suffers from erosion which limits its productivity, does the extension agent's action operate directly on the affected area or on the peasants conditioned by the situation of their region? If his action were to operate directly on the phenomenon or on the problem-situation, in this case, the erosion, without taking into account the human presence of the peasants, the concept of extension would not be applicable. However, the act of extension involves the relationship between human beings and the world in order for human beings to be better equipped to change the world. Thus, the concept of extension which is characterized by the transference of techniques and knowledge is in direct contradiction to a truly humanist outlook.

To return to the linguistic analysis. Modern semantic studies have emphasized the importance of "linguistic fields" in which words interact within a structural relationship of dependence on each other. ("Words form a 'linguistic field' within a conceptual field, expressing a vision of the world which they reconstruct.")[3] Studies have also analyzed the associative relationships which develop within the fields of meaning of various terms. Hence the concept of "associative fields." Analyses of "associative fields" of terms can reveal several different dimensions of the terms. I shall attempt an analysis of this kind, taking the term *extension* as

3. Guiraud, Pierre, op. cit. p. 74.

the subject. By doing this, in seeking to discover the dimensions of its associative field, the following can be derived:

extension .... transmission
extension .... active Subject (who transmits)
extension .... content (chosen by the transmitter)
extension .... recipient (of the content)
extension .... delivering (e.g., in extramural activities—
                something brought by a Subject who is "within
                the wall" to those who are "beyond the wall"
                or "outside the wall").
extension .... messianism (of the extension agent)
extension .... superiority (of the thing given away by the
                person giving away)
extension .... inferiority (of those who receive)
extension .... mechanical transfer (the action of the exten-
                sion agent)
extension .... cultural invasion (through what is brought,
                which reflects the bringers' vision of the world,
                and is imposed on those who passively receive)

It appears that the act of extension, in whatever sector it takes place, means that those carrying it out need to go to "another part of the world" to "normalize it," according to their way of viewing reality: to make it resemble their world. Thus, in its "field of association" the term extension has a significant relation to transmission, handing over, giving, messianism, mechanical transfer, cultural invasion, manipulation, etc. All these terms imply actions which transform people into "things" and negate their existence as beings who transform the world. As we shall see, they further negate the formation and development of real knowledge. They negate the true action and reflection which are the objects of these actions.

It can be argued that this is not the meaning of extension. That extension is educative. It is for this reason that the first critical consideration of this investigation touches on the very concept of extension, on the "field of association" of its meaning. It can be seen clearly from this analysis that the concept of extension does not correspond to an educational undertaking that is liberating. I do not, however, wish to deny the agronomist working in this field the right to be an educator-educatee, with the educatee-educator peasants.[5] Precisely because I am convinced that it is their duty to educate and to be educated, I cannot accept that their work be labeled by a concept which negates it. It could equally well be said that this is a linguistic finesse which cannot change the essence of the extension agent's task. A person who makes such an affirmation both ignores what can be called the operating force of the concepts, and insists on ignoring the real connotation of the term extension. It is this operating force which explains why some extension agents, in defining extension as educative, do not see any contradiction in the statement: "One of the most difficult tasks is to *persuade* the rural masses to accept our propaganda and put these possibilities into practice [this means technical and economic possibilities]. This task is precisely that of the extension agent, whose duty it is to maintain a permanent contact with the rural masses."[6] However worthy the educational intentions of the author just quoted may be—and reading his text inclines one to believe him—it is impossible to deny that for him a fundamental task of the extension agent is "to persuade the rural masses to accept our *propaganda*." It is impossible to affirm that persuasion to accept *propaganda* is an educational activity. I am unable to see how persuasion to accept propaganda can be squared with education: for true education incarnates the permanent search of people together with others for their becoming more fully human in the world in which they exist.

---

5. With regard to the overcoming of the educator-educatee contradiction this produces: there no longer exists the educator of the educatee nor the educatee of the educator but the educator-educatee and the educatee-educator. See Paulo Freire: *Pedagogy of the Oppressed,* Herder and Herder, New York, 1970. (Hereafter referred to as *Pedagogy...*)
6. Willy Timmer: "Planejamento do trabalho de extensão agrícola," Ministry of Agriculture, Agricultural Information Service, Brazil, 1954, p. 24. Italics mine.

In the text quoted, "persuade" and "propaganda" are terms which seem to share a basic connotation which semantically meet in the term "extension." For this reason, "extension" cannot be squared with "education," if the latter is considered "the practice of freedom." The task is not to persuade the peasants to accept propaganda. Whatever its content—commercial, ideological, or technical, propaganda is always used for "domestication."[7]

To persuade implies, fundamentally, a Subject who persuades, in some form or other, and an object on which the act of persuading is exercised. In this case the Subject is the extension agent—the object the peasants. They are the objects of a persuasion which will render them all the more susceptible to propaganda. Neither peasants nor anyone else can be persuaded or forced to submit to the propaganda-myth, if they have the alternative option of liberation. Rather than a passive acceptance of propaganda, liberation implies the problematization of their situation in its concrete objective reality so that being critically aware of it, they can also act critically on it. This, then, is the real work of the agronomists in their role of educators. Agronomists are specialists who work with others on the situation influencing them. However, from a truly humanistic point of view, it is not for them to extend, entrust, or dictate their technical capacities, nor is it for them to persuade by using peasants as "blank pages" for their propaganda. In their role as educators, they must refuse to "domesticate" people. Their task is *communication,* not *extension.*

---

7. domestication: to "domesticate" an animal is to tame it and thereby render it harmless as a household pet. Used metaphorically, "domestication" is the process whereby groups in power seek to channel or neutralize the potentially hostile forces unleashed by the consciousness oppressed peoples have of being exploited by those groups.

b) EXTENSION AND ITS GNOSIOLOGICAL MISINTERPRETATION[8]

It seems clear (the point will be discussed further on) that the basic objective of the extension agent, working on extension, in establishing permanent relationships with peasants, is to try to change their "knowledge" (related to their action on reality) for other knowledge. This other knowledge is that of the extension agent. For a long time agronomists (as technical experts in the relations between human beings and the world) have been aware of the unquestionable importance of their being in close contact with the peasants with the aim of changing the peasants' manner of confronting nature. (Unfortunately agronomists have defined "world" exclusively as "nature"—that which results in production.[9]) To the extent that peasants change their empirical forms of dealing with the land for other forms (those of applied science, that is to say, technical methods), this qualitative change in the process of confronting reality must also produce a change in the results, although not altogether automatically. Rural extension work is thus a specialized activity which is expected to produce these changes.

In the first part of this chapter, I made a semantic analysis of the term extension, and studied the "associative field" of its meaning, thus showing that this term and educational action of a liberating nature are incompatible. Thus the expression "educational extension" only makes sense if it is taken to mean education for the purpose of "domestication." Educating, and educating oneself for the purpose of

---

8. "gnosiology: the theory of the origin, nature, and validity of knowledge; epistemology." *Webster's International Dictionary*, 2nd ed. (1947) p. 1070. (Translator's note)

9. As this study goes on, we shall see how disastrous it is not to be aware of the emergence, from the relationship between human beings and nature, of a strictly and exclusively human world, that of history and culture. This world is being permanently re-created, and in its turn conditions its own creators—who are people—in their manner of confronting the world and of confronting nature. It is not, therefore, possible to understand the relationship between people and nature without investigating the historical-cultural conditioning which governs their way of acting.

liberation, is the task of those who know that they know little (for this very reason they know that they know something and can thus succeed in knowing more) in dialogue with those who almost always think they know nothing. Their aim is that the latter can also know more by the transformation of their thinking that they know nothing into the knowledge that they know little. These initial considerations approach the central theme of the second part of this chapter, in which I will attempt to consider something of importance for the work of the agronomist-educator. I shall discuss the relationships between human beings and the world as basic factors of human knowledge, whatever the category and degree of the knowledge. In doing so I shall indicate the gnosiological misinterpretation to which the term extension leads. For clarification, some repetition is not out of place.

There is in the concept of extension an unquestionably mechanistic connotation, inasmuch as the term implies an action of taking, of transferring, of handing-over, and of depositing something in someone. This something that is being brought, transmitted, transferred (in order finally to be deposited in someone—the peasants), constitutes a group of technical processes, which imply knowledge, which *are* knowledge, and which imply the following questions. Is the act of knowing that by which a subject, transformed into an object, patiently receives content from another? Can this content, which is knowledge *of,* be treated as if it were something static? Is knowledge submitted to historical-sociological conditioning? If a simple conscious awareness of things belonging to the sphere of mere opinion (doxa)[10] does not constitute "absolute" knowledge, how can this sphere be superseded by one in which these things are revealed and the *"raison d'être"* of them touched?

The first gnosiological misinterpretation of extension lies in the following: If there exists a dynamic element in the

---

10. *doxa* and *logos:* in philosophical discourse, *doxa* refers to mere opinion or to an unsubstantiated view, whereas *logos* designates knowledge based on evidence or rational considerations. Both terms are of Greek origin.

practice suggested by such a concept, it is reduced to the act of extending, in which that which is extended becomes static. Consequently, the extending Subjects are active in that they are "actors," in the presence of "spectators" in whom they deposit what they extend.

It could conceivably be said that the work of the agronomist-educator, going by the name of extension, like the work of the agronomist in any other field, is not subject to the type of considerations and analyses which are being made in this study. This affirmation would be explicable only from a narrow, ingenuous, and acritical point of view. The work of the agronomist-educator (which belongs to the domain of the human) contains a philosophical problem which can neither be ignored nor minimized. As in other cases, it is imperative to reflect philosophically. One cannot avoid this, seeing that the basic claim of extension is to substitute one form of knowledge for another. It is sufficient that forms of knowledge be under consideration for philosophical reflection to be required. What is fundamental is that this theoretical reflection should not degenerate into empty verbalism, nor, into a mere explanation of a reality thought to be permanently untouchable. In other words, not reflection in which explanation of the world signifies accepting it as it is, thus transforming knowledge of the world into an instrument for adapting men and women to the world.

When this reflection—although it is barely suggested in this essay—is truly critical, it allows us to understand dialectically the different forms in which human beings *know* in their relations with the world. Because of this, overcoming the ingenuous comprehension of human knowledge which we often retain is made indispensable. This ingenuousness is reflected in educational situations where knowledge of the world is considered as something to be transferred and deposited in the students. This is a static way of looking at knowledge, one which refuses to recognize confrontation with the world as the true source of knowledge with its different levels and phases.

Knowing, whatever its level, is not the act by which a

Subject transformed into an object docilely and passively accepts the contents others give or impose on him or her. Knowledge, on the contrary,[11] necessitates the curious presence of Subjects confronted with the world. It requires their transforming action on reality. It demands a constant searching. It implies invention and re-invention. It claims from each person a critical reflection on the very act of knowing. It must be a reflection which recognizes the knowing process, and in this recognition becomes aware of the "*raison d'être*" behind the knowing and the conditioning to which that process is subject.

Knowing is the task of Subjects, not of objects. It is as a subject, and only as such, that a man or woman can really know. In the learning process the only person who really *learns* is s/he who appropriates what is learned, who apprehends and thereby re-invents that learning; s/he who is able to apply the appropriated learning to concrete existential situations. On the other hand, the person who is filled by another with "contents" whose meaning s/he is not aware of, which contradict his or her way of being in the world, cannot learn because s/he is not challenged. Thus, in a situation of knowing, teacher and student must take on the role of conscious Subjects, mediated by the knowable object that they seek to know. The concept of extension does not allow for this possibility.

This is why those who truly seek to know along with others the meaning of their involvement in this "dialogue" of subjects around a knowable object are not carrying out extension. On the other hand, if they do practice extension, they do not really share with others the conditions for knowing. If their action is merely that of extending elaborated "knowledge" to those who do not possess it, they kill in them the critical capacity for possessing it. The most that

---

11. Erich Fromm: *The Heart of Man*... "Knowledge means that the individual makes his own way, learning, feeling, experimenting with himself, observing others, and finally coming to a conviction without having an 'irresponsible opinion'."

can be done in the extension process, gnosiologically speaking, is to *show* people, without *revelation* or *unveiling*, the existence of a new presence: that of "extended" contents. To capture the awareness of these contents as a simple presence does not make it possible for those who do so to possess real knowledge. Their only being aware of objects as things is merely realization of their existence and does not mean knowledge of them. On the other hand, human beings (who cannot be apprehended without their relations with the world, seeing that they are "beings-in-a-situation") are also beings who work and transform the world. They are beings of "praxis": of action and of reflection. Humans find themselves marked by the results of their own actions in their relations with the world, and through their action on it. By acting they transform; by transforming they create a reality which conditions their manner of acting. Thus it is impossible to dichotomize human beings and the world, since the one cannot exist without the other.

It is through these relations in which they transform and become aware of the presence of things (although this is not true knowing) that mere opinion or "doxa" is developed. Here fact, natural phenomena, things are *presences* of which people are aware, but which are not revealed in their own true interrelationships. Within the sphere of "doxa"[12] in which human beings, we repeat, are ingenuously aware of the presence of things, and of objects, perception of this presence does not mean an "entering into" them, which would result in a critical perception of them. However, objects, facts, events are not isolated presences. One fact is always related to another fact, whether this is obvious or not. The perception of the presence of a fact also comprises the perception of its relations with others. They form one single perception. Thus, the form of perceiving

12. "Although 'doxa' may achieve a state of coherence, it does not imply an objective coherence in things. It does not even aim at being verified, that is, apprehended for rational, non-emotional motives."

Eduardo Nicol: *Los principios de la Ciencia,* Fondo de Cultura Económica, Mexico 1965, p. 44.

facts is not different from the manner of relating them to others. Both are conditioned by the concrete cultural reality in which human being find themselves.

This is what happens in the magic, or preponderantly magic cultures, which are of fundamental interest in that they still constitute the state in which the great majority of peasants of Latin America exist. The relationship between "things perceived" is in no way foreign to the magic way of thinking. Magic perception, which concerns the real and the concrete, is as objective as this relationship; magic thinking, however, is not. This is why, when a people perceive a concrete fact of reality without "entering into" it critically in order to be able to "look at" it from within, faced with the appearance of a mystery, and being unsure of themselves, they assume a magical posture. Finding themselves unable to apprehend the challenge in its authentic relationships with other facts, their tendency (understandably enough) is to go beyond the true relationships to seek an explanation for what is perceived. This happens not only with the natural world but with the historical-social world.

A priest who lives and works in a certain part of the Peruvian plateau told me that there, cold starry nights are a sign of a snowfall which will not be long in coming. When they perceive this sign, the peasants run to the highest point of the village and implore God with desperate cries not to punish them. If hail threatens, the same priest says, peasants make a great fire, and throw pieces of ash into the air, using special rhythms, accompanied by "words of power." Their magic belief, of a syncreto-religious type, is that the hailstones are "produced" by the spirits of those who die without baptism. Hence, the sanction this community imposes on those who do not baptize their children.

In the northeast of Brazil it is usual to combat a plague of lizards by fixing three stakes in the form of a triangle in the place most affected by them. At the end of one of the stakes there is a nail on which the peasant spikes a lizard. He is sure that the remainder will be afraid and withdraw "in procession" between the stakes. While the peasant is waiting for them to go, however, he loses part or all of his crop.

An agronomist told me that in his round of work in a region in the north of Chile he came across a peasant community which was completely helpless in face of the destructiveness of some kind of rodent which was ruining its cultivation. When he asked them what they usually did in such cases, they replied that the first time such a "punishment" had taken place they had been saved by a priest. "How?" asked the agronomist. "He said a few prayers and the rodents fled terrified into the sea where they drowned," they answered.

What can be done from the point of view of education in a peasant community which is at such a level?[13] What can be done with communities which act in this way, whose thought and action—both magic, and conditioned by the structure in which they are situated—hinder their work? How can the practices of these people with regard to nature, based on the magic aspects of their culture, be replaced? The answer cannot lie with those extension agents who, in their relations with the peasants mechanically transfer technical information.

Magic thought is neither illogical nor pre-logical. It possesses its own internal logical structure and opposes as much as possible any new forms mechanically superimposed. Like any other manner of thinking, it is unquestionably bound not only to a way of acting but to a language and a structure. To superimpose on it another form of thought, implying another language, another structure, another manner of acting, stimulates a natural reaction: a defensive reaction in face of the "invader" who threatens its internal equilibrium.

Even when a community which thinks in a predominantly magic way is dominated by the cultural elements which in-

---

13. On the subject of different levels of consciousness, analyses appear in *Education as the Practice of Freedom* in this volume, and in more detail in *Cultural Action for Freedom,* Center for the Study of Development and Social Change, Cambridge, Mass., in collaboration with the Harvard Educational Review, 1970.

vade it, it reveals its resistance to the transformation which these elements bring. The typical form of natural defense takes concrete shape in syncretic expressions. When such communities perceive the foreign cultural elements, they modify them, giving them a kind of "purifying bath." These foreign elements thus retain something of their originality, particularly in their formal aspects, but acquire a new coloration, and a new meaning which the invaded cultural ..-tity imposes on them. It seems important to me to observe the attitude people assume vis-à-vis their natural world, and consequently their cultural and historical world, this probably being an element in what constitutes the magic manner of thinking and acting.

Human beings are active beings, capable of reflection on themselves and on the activity in which they are engaged. They are able to detach themselves from the world in order to find their place in it and with it. Only people are capable of this act of "separation" in order to find their place in the world and enter in a critical way into their own reality. "To enter into" reality means to look at it objectively, and apprehend it as one's field of action and reflection. It means to penetrate it more and more lucidly in order to discover the true interrelations between the facts observed.

However, the more we observe the behavior patterns and the thought-habits of peasants, the more we can conclude that in certain areas (to a greater or lesser degree) they come so close to the natural world that they feel more *part* of this world than transformers of the world. There exists between them and their natural world (and obviously their cultural world) a strong "umbilical cord" which binds them.[14] This nearness which identifies them with the natural world makes the act of "entering into" it difficult for them, inasmuch as the nearness does not allow them to see in perspective that which they "enter into." A mistaken apprehension of what links one fact to another, induces a likewise

14. See Cândido Mendes: *Memento dos Vivos,* Editóra Tempo Brasileiro, Rio de Janeiro, 1969.

erroneous understanding of the facts. This, in its turn, is associated with magic action.

In situations in which "becoming aware of reality," of the elements which constitute it, takes an "entering into" form rather than a "belonging to" form, in situations in which the level of certitude and success is already assured by experience, magical formulae are despised.[15] What cannot be denied is that whether we are dealing with pure "doxa," or whether we are dealing with magic thought, we find ourselves faced with ingenuous forms of apprehending objective reality. We are faced with simple forms of pre-scientific knowledge. The gnosiological misinterpretation of the term "extension" will not be helpful in collaborating with the peasants with the aim of substituting a predominantly critical form of acting for their magic ways. Extension as an act of transference can of itself do nothing or almost nothing in this sense.

Frequently the mere presence of new objects in a community, of a new method, of a different way of acting, produces mistrust and total or partial rejection. They can also be accepted. It cannot be denied that when the level of perception of the world (conditioned by the very social structure in which men and women exist) is maintained, these new objects, methods, or forms of acting, can also, as cultural manifestations which are foreign to the culture into which they have penetrated, be magically perceived.[16] Hence, they may undergo a distortion in the new context to which they were "extended."

The question is thus not as simple as it might appear. Substituting "elaborated" techniques for magic ways of acting involves cultural aspects and levels of perception which make up the social structure. It involves problems of lan-

---

15. See Bronislaw Malinovski: *Magic, Science and Religion,* Anchor Books, New York, 1967.
16. Even in the case in which the transformations take place suddenly, for example, through a process of accelerated industrialization, where there is no associated cultural action process in which there is a tendency to supersede magic forms of behavior, many of the latter are retained, simply taking a different form of expression according to the new elements brought in, while others crystallize into traditions.

guage, which cannot be separated from thought, just as thought and language cannot be separated from structure. In whatever moment of history a social structure exists (whether it is undergoing a rapid transformation or not) the main task of the agronomist-educator (which is easier in the first case) is to attempt to overcome the magic perception of reality, simultaneously achieving technical training. At the same time it must overcome the "doxa" by the "logos" of reality. It is the attempt to extend knowledge which is largely sensuous to knowledge which, taking its departure from the sensuous, touches the *raison d'être* of reality.

The more one approaches the objective, challenging *raison d'être* of reality through action and reflection, the more one can reveal it by entering into it. Thus, to substitute our "elaborated" techniques for the empirical manner of acting of the peasants is at once an anthropological, epistemological, and structural problem. This means that it cannot be solved through the gnosiological misinterpretation to which the concept of "extension" leads.

Any attempt at mass education, whether associated with professional training or not, whether in the agricultural sphere or in the urban and industrial field, must (for the reasons just analyzed) possess a basic aim: to make it possible for human beings, through the problematizing of the unity being-world (or of human beings in their relations with the world and with other human beings) to penetrate more deeply the *prise de conscience* of the reality in which they exist. This deepening of the *prise de conscience*, which must develop in the action which transforms reality, produces with this action an overlaying of basically sensuous knowledge of reality with that which touches the *raison d'être* of this reality. People take over the position they have in their *here* and *now*. This results (and at the same time it produces this) in their discovering their own presence within a totality, within a structure, and not as "imprisoned" or "stuck to" the structure or its parts. When they do not perceive reality as the totality within which the different parts interact, they lose themselves in a "focalist" vision of it. Merely to perceive reality partially deprives them of the possibility of a genuine action *on* reality.

It should be said in passing that this is one of the errors of various efforts made in the organization and development of communities, and also in so-called "leader-training." This is the error of not seeing reality as a totality. This error is repeated, for example, in attempts to train peasants by adopting an ingenuous attitude to the problem of techniques. That is, when it is not made obvious that techniques do not just happen. That polished or "elaborated" techniques, like the science of which they are a practical application, are socio-historically conditioned. Techniques cannot be neutral.

On the other hand, the knowledge of the peasants, which is by nature experiential (it cannot be otherwise) is equally conditioned. For example, their attitudes towards erosion, reforestation, seedtime or harvest (precisely because they are part of a structure and not isolated units) have a relation to peasant attitudes to religion, to the cult of the dead, to the illness of animals, etc. All these aspects are contained within a cultural totality. As a structure, this cultural totality reacts as a whole. If one of its parts is affected, an automatic reflex occurs in the others. A solidarity exists between the various dimensions which constitute a cultural structure. This solidarity, within which these various dimensions exist, produces different reactions to the presence of the new elements introduced into it. Any reaction has its own "frame of reference." If any dimensional unity is threatened, the fact is passed on to another, closely related to it. This relation may not always be visible, and may be obscure rather than clear. This can be seen when there is an attempt to modify techniques governed by beliefs. The same happens when beliefs are threatened, beliefs which for their part determine methods of action and forms of behavior.[17]

17. A North American sister told us that in some regions of the Peruvian high plateau, particularly subject to lightning, the peasants all go to chapel on Sunday morning "to hear Mass." She added that, on various occasions, she saw groups of young peasants in front of a wooden statue of a horse

It is thus not possible for the agronomist-educator to attempt to change these attitudes (knowledge of these—and this cannot be ignored—occurs principally at the level of the senses) unless s/he is familiar with their view of the world, and unless s/he takes it as a whole. On the same level as the problematic discussion of erosion and reforestation, for example, the critical involvement of the peasants with their reality as a whole is imperative. To discuss erosion (in the problematizing dialogical conception of education) erosion must appear to the peasants in their "basic view" as a real problem, as a "distinct perception" firmly related to other problems. Erosion is not merely a natural problem, since the response to it, taking it as a challenge, is cultural. Indeed, the mere facing-up to the world by men and women is in a way already a cultural action. Because the answers peasants give to natural challenges are cultural, they cannot be replaced by superimposing the equally cultural responses (ours) that we "extend" to them.

Knowledge is not *extended* from those who consider that they know to those who consider that they do not know. Knowledge is built up in the relations between human beings and the world, relations of transformation, and perfects itself in the critical problematization of these relations. In order to discuss any kind of technical question with peasants, they must see this question as a "distinct perception." If it is not this, it must become this. Whether it is a "dis-

---

with St. James proudly astride it, saying something she could not make out.

"It seemed to me," the sister told us, "that they were speaking not only to St. James, but also to his horse."

One day, a priest who had just come to the village, and who declared that this behavior on the part of the peasants was a superstition prejudicial to the Catholic faith, removed from the chapel the object he considered to be profaning it. He placed St. James and his horse in the courtyard outside the chapel. When the peasants saw what had happened, they held a sort of council, and immediately invaded the chapel and destroyed nearly everything in it.

They recuperated St. James and his horse and re-installed them in their old place, and held a big procession in the main square of the village. For them, St. James was a sort of "lord of the lightnings...."

If anyone offended him (worse still, if they removed him) and no one came to his defense, this could bring down the anger of the saint who would make the curse of the lightning fall on them.... The priest nearly paid very dearly for his sectarianism and for his ignorance of anthropology.

tinct perception" or not, the peasants still must in both cases apprehend the interplay of relations between the "distinct perception" and other dimensions of reality.

The effort required is not one of *extension* but of *conscientização*. If it is successfully carried out, it allows individuals to assume critically the position they have in relation to the rest of the world. The critical taking up of this position brings them to assume the true role incumbent on them as people. This is the role of being Subjects in the transformation of the world, which humanizes them. The work of agronomists thus cannot be the schooling or even the training of peasants in techniques of ploughing, sowing, harvesting, reforesting, etc. If they limit themselves to a simple form of training, they can in certain circumstances obtain a better work-output. However, they will have contributed nothing (or nearly nothing) to the development of peasants as people. This means that the concept of *extension*, analyzed from a semantic viewpoint, and from that of its gnosiological misinterpretation, does not square with the indispensable technical and humanistic work which it is the agronomist's duty to carry out.

Chapter II

a) EXTENSION AND CULTURAL INVASION— A NECESSARY CRITICISM

The analysis I propose to make in this chapter requires some prior considerations, considerations which revolve around a theme whose extension is easily recognized. These will be presented summarily, sufficient only to clarify the basic observations I shall make. The considerations concern a theory of action based on anti-dialectics, which is a theory of action diametrically opposed to one stemming from dialectics.[1]

To begin with, only human beings, that is, beings who work, who possess a thought-language, who act and who are capable of reflection on themselves and on their own action (such actions becoming separate entities), only they are beings of praxis. They *are* praxis. Only they are beings of relations in a world of relations.[2] Their presence in this world, a presence which is a *being with*, comprises a permanent confrontation of the human being with the world. Detaching themselves from their surroundings, they transform their environment. They do not merely adapt to it. Humans are consequently beings of decision.[3] Detachment from one's environment can only be achieved in relation with that environment. Human beings are human because they exist in and with the world. This *existing* implies a permanent relation to the world as well as an action on it. This world, be-

---

1. See *Pedagogy of the Oppressed*, Herder and Herder, New York, 1970, in which I discuss this question in full.
2. On man as a being of *relations* and animals as beings of *contacts*, and the connotations of these concepts, see *Education as the Practice of Freedom*, in this volume.
3. The term "decision" comes from "to decide" from the Latin *decidere*: to cut. In the text, following its etymology, the term "decision" means the "cutting" people perform to separate themselves from the natural world while continuing in the world. The operation of "entering into" the world is implicit in *decision*.

cause it is a world of history and culture, is a world of men and women—not simply a world of "nature."

Human actions in the world are conditioned by their own results, by their own outcome. Thus there are different degrees of relations to the world, different degrees of action and perception. Nevertheless, whatever the degree of action on the world, it implies a theory. Even those actions called magic are governed by theory.[4]

We must have a clear and lucid grasp of our action (which implies a theory) whether we wish to or not. Instead of the mere "doxa" of the action we perform, we must go right to its "logos." That is the specific task of philosophical reflection.[5] The role of this reflection is to react to the action and to reveal its objectives, its means, and its efficacy. When this is done, what perhaps previously did not appear as the theory of action, is now revealed as such. If there is no dichotomy between theory and practice, reflection on our actions reveals the theory—without which the action (or practice) is not a true one. The practice in turn acquires a new significance when it is illustrated by a theory.

I shall try to show in this chapter that the theory implicit in the action of extending, in extension, is anti-dialogical. As such, it is incompatible with true education.[6] The anti-dialogue nature of the term "extension" emerges clearly from the analyses made in the first two parts of this essay where it was studied semantically and its gnosiological misinterpretation discussed. Anti-dialogue and dialogue are embodied

---

4. "The magic art is directed towards the attainment of practical ends; like any other art or craft it is also governed by theory, and by a system of principles which dictate the manner in which the act has to be performed in order to be effective. Thus, magic and science show a number of similarities and with Sir James Frazer, we can appropriately call magic a pseudo science." Malinowski, Bronislaw, *op. cit.* p. 140.

5. The philosophy of science, or of techniques, is not the pastime of those who do nothing. Nor is it a waste of time, as technocrats—if not technicians —may imagine.

See also footnote 10, Chapter I of this study.

6. This does not mean that all agronomists (or so-called extension agents) are necessarily anti-dialogical. It simply means that if and when they engage in dialogue they cannot practice rural extension. If they participate in rural extension they cannot engage in dialogue.

in contradictory forms of action; the latter in turn imply equally irreconcilable theories. Some of these forms of action interact in an anti-dialogical sense, others in a dialogical sense. Thus, the factor which distinguishes an action of anti-dialogue cannot be a constitutive element of an action of dialogue and vice versa.

Among the various characteristics of the anti-dialogical theory of action, I have chosen to consider one: cultural invasion. Any invasion implies, of course, an invading Subject. His cultural-historical situation which gives him his vision of the world is the environment from which he starts out. He seeks to penetrate another cultural-historical situation and impose his system of values on its members. The invader reduces the people in the situation he invades to mere objects of his action.

The relationships between invader and invaded are situated at opposite poles. They are relationships of authority.[7] The invader acts, the invaded are under the illusion that they are acting through the action of the other; the invader has his say;[8] the invaded, who are forbidden this, listen to what the invader says. The invader thinks, at most, *about* the invaded, never *with* them; the latter have their thinking done for them by the former. The invader dictates; the invaded patiently accept what is dictated. For the cultural invasion to be effective, and for the cultural invader to attain his objectives, the action must be supported by other complementary actions, ones which constitute different dimensions of the anti-dialogue theory. Thus, any cultural invasion presupposes conquest, manipulation, and messianism on the part of the invader. It presupposes propaganda which domesticates rather than liberates. Since cultural invasion is

7. Authoritarianism need not necessarily be associated with physical repression. It can also be seen in actions based on the "argument of authority." "This is the right way—it's technically correct—don't raise questions, just do it."
8. For having one's say, and the meaning of this act, see Paulo Freire: *La Alfabetisación de Adultos: la crítica de su vision ingénua y la comprensión de su vision crítica.* Ernani, Maria Fiori: *Aprender a decir su palabra—el Método de Alfabetisación del Profesor Paulo Freire,* Santiago, 1968.

an act of conquest *per se,* it needs further conquest to sustain itself.

Propaganda, slogans, myths are the instruments employed by the invader to achieve his objectives: to persuade those invaded that they must be the objects of his action, that they must be the docile prisoners of his conquest. Thus it is incumbent on the invader to destroy the character of the culture which has been invaded, nullify its form, and replace it with the byproducts of the invading culture.

The manipulation[9]—never the organization—of the individuals belonging to the invaded culture is another integral feature of the anti-dialogical theory of action. As a form of leadership which exploits the emotions of the people, manipulation inculcates into the invaded the illusion of acting or their acting within the action of the manipulators. In that manipulation encourages "massification"[10] it categorically contradicts the affirmation by human beings as Subjects. Such affirmation can only occur when those who are engaged in a transforming action upon reality also make their own choices and decisions. In fact manipulation and conquest, as expressions of cultural invasion, are never means for liberation. They are always means for "domestication."

True humanism, which serves human beings, cannot ac-

---

9. Manipulation is a typical feature of those societies which undergo the process of historical transition, from the "closed" type of society to an "open" one in which the presence of the emerging masses makes itself felt. In the preceding stage of the process, the masses are "submerged" in society. But when they emerge from the transition they undergo a change of attitude: from being mere spectators they insist on participation and a share in running affairs. These circumstances produce the phenomenon of populism which is the answer to the emergence of the masses. Populist leadership, as a part of the action of manipulation, becomes the mediator between the emerging masses and the oligarchic elites.
10. By "massification" I do not mean the process of the emergence of the masses (referred to in the previous note), which results in their search to affirm themselves and participate historically (society of masses), but a state in which people do not make their own decisions although they may think that they do.

"Massification" is dehumanization and alienation.

The "irrational" and the "myth" are always associated with "massification."

The same meaning is implied in phrases such as "mass society," "mass man," "the faceless crowd," etc.

cept manipulation under any name whatsoever. For humanism there is no path other than dialogue. To engage in dialogue is to be genuine. For true humanism, to engage in dialogue is not to engage without commitment. Humanism is to make dialogue live. Dialogue is not to invade, not to manipulate, not to "make slogans." It is to devote oneself to the constant transformation of reality. In that dialogue is the content of the form of being which is peculiarly human, it is excluded from all relationships in which people are transformed into "beings for another" by people who are false "beings for themselves." Dialogue cannot imprison itself in any antagonistic relationship. Dialogue is the loving encounter of people, who, mediated by the world, "proclaim" that world. They transform the world and in transforming it, humanize it for all people. This encounter in love cannot be an encounter of irreconcilables.

Cultural invasion through dialogue cannot exist. There is no such thing as dialogical manipulation or conquest.[11] These terms are mutually exclusive. Although I have said that not all agronomists who are called extension agents practice cultural invasion, it is not possible to ignore the ostensible suggestion of cultural invasion in the term "extension."

This is not a pointless argument. The moment social workers define their work as *assistencialism*[12] and yet say that it is educational, they commit a mistake which has fatal consequences. In the same way, when linguists say they are "functionalists," they cannot, as "functionalists," state that language is a system of relationships. Similarly, those who

---

11. *Conquista* (conquest): feminine participle of the old form *conquerir:* to conquer. Latin: *conquirere:* to seek everywhere. It is not necessary to seek people everywhere. On the contrary one should *be* with them.
  The conquest implicit in dialogue is the conquest of the world for the becoming more fully human of all human beings.
12. *assistencialism:* a term used in Latin America to describe policies of financial or social "assistance" which attack symptoms, but not causes, of social ills. It has overtones of paternalism, dependency, and a "hand-out" approach. It contrasts with "promocionalismo" which, on the contrary, "promotes" people to a state of vigorous self-capacity to solve their own problems.

reduce all objectivity to human beings and their conscious-ness[13] (including the existence of other human beings) can-not discuss the dialectic of Subjectivity-objectivity. They cannot accept the existence of a concrete, objective world with which human beings are involved in a permanent rela-tionship. If a social worker (in the broadest sense) supposes that s/he is "*the* agent of change," it is with difficulty that s/he will see the obvious fact that, if the task is to be really educational and liberating, those with whom s/he works cannot be the objects of her actions. Rather, they too will be agents of change.[14] If social workers cannot perceive this, they will succeed only in manipulating, steering and "domes-ticating." If on the other hand they recognize others, as well as themselves, as agents of change, they will cease to have the exclusive title of "*the* agent of change."

This then is the dilemma of agronomists and extension agents, in the face of which they must be critically aware. If, in accordance with the concept of extension, they trans-form their specialized knowledge and methods into some-thing static and materialized and extend them mechanically to the peasants—invading the peasant culture and view of the world—they deny that men and women are beings who make decisions. If, however, agronomists affirm their knowl-edge through dialogical work, they neither invade, manipu-late, nor conquer. They thus deny the connotation of the term "extension."

There is one argument, with which I wish to deal, that has frequently emerged in the study-encounters that I have had with agronomist-extension agents. This argument is presented as if it were indestructibly basic to explain the need for an anti-dialogical action on the part of agronomists vis-à-vis peasant communities. It refers to the question of time, or to use the usual technical expression, "time-wast-ing." For many, if not the majority of agronomists with

---

13. The idealist theory of subjectivity known as solipsism; Latin: *solo:* only, *ipsé:* same.
14. For this, see Paulo Freire: "The Role of the Social Worker in the Process of Change," in *Sobre la Accion Cultural,* ICIRA, Chile, 1970.

whom I have participated in seminars dealing with the aspects I have raised in this study, "dialogue is not viable. This is because its results are slow, uncertain and long-drawn-out." "Its slowness," say others, "in spite of the results it may produce, is at odds with the urgent need of the country to stimulate production." "Thus," they affirm emphatically, "this time-wasting cannot be justified. In choosing between dialogue and anti-dialogue, we accept the latter as it is more rapid." There are even those who are so influenced by the urgency of time as to clearly state that "it is important to make 'deposits' of technical knowledge in the peasants, so that they will rapidly be able to replace empirical habits with appropriate modern techniques." "We are faced," say others, "with a very worrying problem—that of production-increase. How can we possibly waste so much time attempting to fit our actions into the framework of the cultural conditions of the peasants? How can we waste so much time on dialogue with them?" "There is an even more serious point," others announce. "How can we dialogue about technical affairs? How can we dialogue with peasants about a technical method they are not familiar with?" "Dialogue would be possible if its theme concerned their daily life, and did not deal with technical methods."

In the face of the concerns and the questions (which are in fact categorical affirmations) thus expressed, I think that there can be no doubt that we are confronted with the defense of cultural invasion as the sole solution of the agronomist. It is important that I take the time to analyze these affirmations, which are almost always presented or expressed in the form of questions.

Firstly, it is not difficult to see that these questions reflect the gnosiological misinterpretation implicit in the term extension and discussed in the first chapter. They unquestionably reveal a false conception of the way knowledge is acquired. For the extension agent knowledge is the result of the act of depositing contents into "empty consciousness."[15]

---

15. See *Pedagogy of the Oppressed,* op. cit

The more active the person who deposits, the more passive and docile those who receive, the more comprehension there will be. Within this misconception, these affirmations suggest ignorance of the historical-sociological conditions for knowledge to which I have referred several times. Their authors forget that although the rural areas receive urban influences through radio, and although communication is made easier by the construction of roads that diminish distances, nevertheless they still retain their basic forms of being. These rural forms differ from urban ones even with regard to the manner of walking, of dressing, of speaking, and of eating. This does not mean that people cannot change. It simply means that such changes are not mechanical ones.

In my opinion such affirmations express an unjustified lack of faith in people, an underestimation of their power of reflection, of their ability to take on the true role of seekers of knowledge: that of the Subjects of this search. Hence the tendency to transform them into objects of the "knowledge" imposed on them. Hence the haste to make them the docile and patient recipients of "communiqués" which are inected into them, while on the contrary the act of knowing and of learning requires of people an impatient, unquiet, indocile attitude. It requires a seeking, which, inasmuch as it *is* a seeking, cannot be reconciled with the static attitude of one who merely acts as the depository of the contents delivered by another.

This lack of faith in people in turn reveals another error: the assertion that their ignorance is absolute. Such an assertion is always associated with an ingenuous conception of knowledge as a deposit. If people are assumed to be absolutely ignorant, there must be people who think of them in this way. The latter, the subjects of this definition, naturally classify themselves as those who know. By affirming the absolute ignorance of others, they reveal their own ignorance. This means that they practice what I call the "alienation of ignorance." This supposes that ignorance is always present in others, never in the person who "alienates."

In fact, it is enough that we recognize that men and women are beings who are in permanent relation with the world which they transform through their work to be aware of them as beings who know, although this knowledge is manifested at different levels: of "doxa," of magic, and of "logos," which is true knowledge. In spite of all this, or perhaps because of it, neither ignorance nor knowledge can be absolute. No one can know everything, just as no one can be ignorant of everything. Knowledge begins with the awareness of knowing little (in the function of which one acts). And knowing that they know little, people are prepared to know more. If we possessed absolute knowledge, this knowledge could not exist because it would not be in a state of being. A person who knew everything would not be able to continue knowing because s/he would never ask anything. Human beings constantly create and re-create their knowledge, in that they are inconclusive, historical beings engaged in a permanent act of discovery. All new knowledge is generated from knowledge which has become old, which in its turn had been generated from previous knowledge. Thus, knowledge is in constant succession, such that all new knowledge, when it is established as such, becomes the basis for the knowledge which will replace it.

What can be said about the affirmation that dialogue is not viable principally because it implies a waste of time? What are the empirical facts behind this very categorical affirmation, which results in those who make it choosing to donate or to impose their techniques?

Let us suppose, for the sake of argument, that all those who make such an affirmation have already tried dialogical experiments with the peasants. Let us also suppose that these experiments were carried out according to the principles which lie behind true dialogue. That the group dynamic sought was not attempted by manipulative techniques and that despite everything dialogue was difficult, and participation nearly or entirely non-existent. Even in that event, should one conclude that dialogue is not viable and accept that such a strategy is a waste of time? Have we asked, investigated, and sought to know the reasons why peasants remain silent and apathetic in the face of our attempts at dialogue with them? Where else can one seek these reasons but in the historical, sociological, and cultural conditions which condition them?

Continuing, for the sake of argument, to suppose the above hypotheses to be true, I must assert that peasants do not refuse to dialogue because they are by nature opposed to dialogue. There are historical-sociological, cultural, and structural reasons for their refusal. Their existential experience is constituted within the limits of anti-dialogue. The *latifundist*[16] structure, which is colonial by nature, enables the landlord (because of strength and prestige) to extend his "possession" over the people as well as over the land. This "possession" of the people, who are more or less "reified," is expressed through an interminable series of limitations which diminish their field of free acting. Even when the personality of a more humane land-owner lends itself to the establishing of relations of affection between the land-owner and his "tenants," the "social distance" between them is still not eliminated. Closeness of an affective type between persons of different "social status" does not diminish the distance imposed by and implicit in the "status." In this affective closeness one should observe not only the "humanitarianism" of an individual but also the structure in which s/he is placed and by which s/he is conditioned. This is why the latifundiary structure cannot transform the humanitarianism of a few into the true humanism of all.

In this rigid, vertical structure of relationships there is no real room for dialogue. It is within these same rigid vertical relations that the peasant consciousness is historically developed. This is the consciousness of the oppressed. With no experience of dialogue, with no experience of participation, the oppresed are often unsure of themselves. They have consistently been denied their right to have their say, having historically had the duty to only listen and obey.

---

16. See definition for *latifundium* p. 15

It is thus normal that they almost always maintain an attitude of mistrust towards those who attempt to dialogue with them. Actually, this distrustful attitude is directed also toward themselves. They are not sure of their own ability. They are influenced by the myth of their own ignorance. It is understandable that they prefer not to engage in dialogue, that after fifteen or twenty minutes of active participation, they say to the educator: "Excuse us, sir, we who don't know should keep quiet and listen to you who know."[17] Those who declare dialogue to be impossible will probably say that these observations only serve to reinforce their hypotheses. This is not true. What these considerations clearly reveal is that the difficulty of dialogue with peasants does not arise because they are peasants, but comes from the social structure, in that it is "permanent" and oppressive.

A more serious question would be the investigation of the possibility of dialogue as long as there is no change in the *latifundiary* structure; since it is in this structure that the explanation of the silence of the peasants lies. This silence begins in one way or another to disappear in areas undergoing agrarian reform or subject to the indirect influence of such areas, as I observed in Chile. Be this as it may, whether agronomists experience many or few difficulties, it will not be with anti-dialogue that the silence of the peasants will be broken, but with a dialogue in which this very silence and its causes are presented as a problem. The work of the agronomist as educator is not confined, and should not be confined to the domain of techniques. For techniques do not exist without men and women, and men and women do not exist apart from history, apart from the reality they have to transform.

The difficulties which hierarchical structures, to a greater or lesser degree, impose in the task of dialogue, do not justify anti-dialogue—of which cultural invasion is a direct consequence. However serious the difficulties, those who are

---

17. Referred to by Alvaro Manriquez, of the *Institute for Agricultural and Livestock Development* (INDAP) in one of his presentations on the psychosocial method among Chilean peasants.

committed to human beings, to their cause and to their liberation cannot indulge in anti-dialogue.[18] These are the difficulties which cause agronomists—and not only agronomists
—to talk of lost time or of the time wasted in dialogue.
This is the loss of time that would be harmful to the success
of the objectives of a program to increase production. Such
an increase in production, it is argued, is vital for the nation. It would of course be ingenuous not to emphasize the
importance of production. But what can be said—and the
reader will allow me to state the obvious—is that agricultural production does not exist in a vacuum. It is a result
of the relations between human beings and nature (prolonged into the relations between human beings and their
historical-cultural dimension), the conditions of which we
have already discussed several times in this essay. If agricultural production were concerned merely with things, and
had nothing to do with the confrontation of human beings
and their world, there would be no need for dialogue. (And
this would be so just because it is only through human beings
that things have their place in time; from human beings
they acquire an accepted and a meaningful significance.
Things neither communicate nor recount.) But this cannot
be the case for people, who are historical beings, able to
give an autobiography of themselves. From a human point
of view, lost time is that in which people are "reified."[19]
Lost time, even time which gives the illusion of having been
saved, is time spent in bla-bla-bla, in verbalism, just as pure
activism is also time lost; neither constitutes the time of
true praxis.

Time spent on dialogue should not be considered wasted

---

18. Regarding dialogical work on structures which have not been transformed, see Paulo Freire: a) "The Role of the Social Worker in the Process
of Change," in *Sobre la Acción Cultural, op. cit.* b) "The Duty of the Professional Towards Society." See further, Ernani, Maria Fiori: "Aprender a
decir su palabra—el Método de Alfabetisación del Profesor Paulo Freire."
op. cit.
19. However, from a concrete, realist viewpoint, which is not strictly ethical,
it is not lost time, since it is precisely from this that the new "time," with
its new dimensions, in which people will triumph over their human condition, is generated.

time. It presents problems and criticizes, and in criticizing, gives human beings their place within their own reality as the true transforming Subjects of reality. Even when we regard the work of the agronomist-educator as limited to no more than the teaching of new techniques, there is no comparison between dialogue and anti-dialogue. Any delay caused by dialogue—in reality a fictitious delay—means time saved in firmness, in self-confidence, and confidence in others, which anti-dialogue cannot offer.

Let me consider finally the statement which asserts that dialogue is not possible if the information to be transmitted is of a scientific or technical kind. This includes all "knowledge" that is beyond the historical experience of the recipients. It is always said that it is impossible to dialogue with peasants about agricultural techniques,[20] just as it is impossible in the primary school to dialogue, for example, about the fact that 4×4 cannot be 15. Similarly it is said to be impossible to create a dialogue with pupils about a historical fact, which took place at a certain time and in a certain way. The only thing for the educator to do is to recount the facts, which must then be memorized. There is certainly an error in these doubts which, as I have said, are almost always in fact affirmations. In many cases, this error is possibly the result of a failure to understand what dialogue is, what knowledge is, and how both are constituted. The use of dialogue does not require that the pupil retrace each of the

---

20. However, agricultural techniques are not foreign to the peasants. Their daily work is a confrontation with the land, preparing it and cultivating it. This takes place within the limits of their experience, that is, within the limits of their culture.

It is not only a matter of teaching them, but also of learning from them. It would be difficult for an experienced and receptive agronomist not to gain some benefit from living with the peasants. If dialogue reveals the structural difficulties I have already analyzed, anti-dialogue will encounter greater difficulties still. The former is able to overcome inherent difficulties by posing them as problems to be confronted by both the peasants and the agent. The latter by its very nature cannot represent the difficulties in this way. It has to substitute the methods of the agent for the empirical methods of the peasants. Since successful substitution requires critical acts of decision (which anti-dialogue does not engender) it results in the mere superposition of planned methods on the empirical methods of the peasants.

steps taken historically in the growth of scientific and technical knowledge. Nor does it require that students guess or indulge in a purely intellectual game of empty words. Dialogue in any situation (whether it involves scientific and technical knowledge, or experiential knowledge) demands the problematic confrontation of that very knowledge in its unquestionable relationship with the concrete reality in which it is engendered, and on which it acts, in order to better understand, explain, and transform that reality. The fact that 4×4 is 16 and that this is only true in a given system does not mean that the pupil ought simply to memorize that 4×4 is 16. The objectivity of this truth in one system has to be shown problematically. Actually, 4×4 would be a false abstraction if it were not related to reality, especially as learned by a child. In a table to be learned by heart 4×4 is one thing; 4×4 translated into concrete experience is another: e.g., making four bricks four times. Instead of mechanically memorizing 4×4, the pupil ought to discover its relation to something in human life.

This scientific task requires discussion—the historical dimension of knowledge, its placing in time, its instrumentality. All this is a subject of investigation and dialogue. Thus an historical fact cannot just be recounted with an exaggerated delight in the details of dates, and reduced to something static to be put on a calendar and fixed. If it is not possible to abstain from talking about what happened and how it happened, the fact itself must be stated problematically for the pupils. They must reflect on the "wherefore" of the fact and on its connection with other facts in an overall context. It could be said that the task of the history teacher is to situate isolated historical facts in their totality, to "explain' history. For me the task is something different: it is to present the material in such a way as to encourage students to think critically so that they might give their own interpretations to the data.

If education is dialogical, it is clear that the role of the teacher is important, whatever the situation. As s/he dialogues with the pupils, s/he must draw their attention to points that are unclear or naïve, always looking at them problematically. Why? How? Is it so? What relation is there between the statement you have just made, and that of your companion? Is there any contradiction between them? Why? It can be said once more that such an approach needs time. That often there is "no time to lose," "there is a syllabus to be completed." Once again in the name of time which is not to be wasted, time is wasted. Young people are alienated by the kind of copybook thought that is almost entirely verbally narrated. Moreover, the content of what is narrated must be passively received and then memorized for repetition later. Dialogue does not depend on the content which is to be seen problematically. Everything can be presented problematically.

The role of the educator is not to "fill" the educatee with "knowledge," technical or otherwise. It is rather to attempt to move towards a new way of thinking in both educator and educatee, through the dialogical relationships between both. The flow is in both directions. The best student in physics or mathematics, at school or university, is not one who memorizes formulae but one who is aware of the reason for them. For students, the more simply and docilely they receive the contents with which their teachers "fill" them in the name of knowledge, the less they are able to think and the more they become merely repetitive. The best philosophy student is not one who discourses, "ipsis verbis," on the philosophy of Plato, Marx, or Kant but one who thinks critically about their ideas and takes the risk of thinking too. No philosophers, no scientists, develop their thought or systematize their scientific knowledge without being challenged and confronted by problems. While this does not mean that a person who is challenged automatically or necessarily becomes a philosopher or a scientist, it does mean that challenge is basic to the constitution of knowledge. Thus, when a scientist in search of one thing discovers something else, something not anticipated (this happens continually) the discovery originates in the attempt to solve a problem.

It is this that I defend: if scientific knowledge and the formulation of disciplined thought cannot be separated from a problematic approach, then the apprehension of this scientific knowledge and of this disciplined philosophical thought cannot be separated from a problematic approach to the very learning which the educatee must absorb. I sometimes have the impression (without being dogmatic) that many of those who express doubts about this rationalize their lack of belief in people and in dialogue through defense mechanisms. Their aim, basically, is to continue to be "banking" dissertators and invaders. This fear of dialogue needs, however, to be justified. The best way to do this is to rationalize it, by talking about its non-viability and about "time-wasting." This means that between the "distributors" of erudite knowledge and their pupils, there can never be dialogue. For those who think in this way, anti-dialogue is essential in the name of "cultural continuity." This continuity exists. Precisely because it is continuity, it is a process and not a paralysis. Culture only *is* as long as it continues to be. It endures only because it changes. Perhaps it would be better to say: culture only "lasts" when it is part of the contradictory interplay of permanence and change.

Those who fear dialogue prefer lengthy and erudite discourses full of quotations. Instead of problem-posing dialogue, they prefer a so-called "reading-control" (which is a form of controlling the students rather than the reading). This does not result in any kind of creative intellectual discipline, only in the subjugation of the educatee to the text, the reading of which has to be "controlled." Sometimes this is called evaluation. Alternatively it is asserted that young people should be "made to study," or "forced to know." Such educators have no wish to run the risk of adventuring into dialogue, the risk incurred by problem-posing. They retreat into their discursive and rhetorical classes, which have a lulling effect on students. Enjoying the narcissistic pleasure of the sound of their own words, they lull the critical capacity of the educatee to sleep.

Dialogue and problem-posing never lull anyone to sleep.

Dialogue awakens an awareness. Within dialogue and problem-posing educator-educatee and educatee-educator go forward together to develop a critical attitude. The result of this is the perception of the interplay of knowledge and all its adjuncts. This knowledge reflects the world; reflects human beings in and with the world explaining the world. Even more important it reflects having to justify their transformation of the world. Problem-posing supersedes the old "magister dixit" behind which those who regard themselves as the "proprietors," "administrators," or "bearers" of knowledge attempt to hide themselves. To reject problem-posing dialogue at any level is to maintain an unjustifiable pessimism towards human beings and to life. It is to lapse back into the practice of depositing false knowledge which anaesthetizes the critical spirit, contributes to the "domesticating" of human beings, and makes cultural invasion possible.

b) AGRARIAN REFORM, CULTURAL TRANSFORMATION, AND THE ROLE OF THE AGRONOMIST-EDUCATOR

I said in the first part of this chapter that the work of the agronomist-educator cannot be limited to the substituion of new methods for the empirical practices of the peasants. There are two fundamental reasons which lead me to make this statement. One is that it is impossible to change technical practices without repercussions in other areas of human existence. The other is that neutral education cannot exist—in whatever field. In the second part of this chapter I analyze the role of the agronomist in the process of agrarian reform, without dichotomizing technology and culture.

To put it concretely, agronomists cannot reduce their actions to a non-existent neutrality as if technicians were isolated from the wider universe in which they exist as human beings. From the moment in which they enter and participate in the system of relationships between human beings and nature, their work takes on a broader perspective in which the technical training of the peasants becomes one with other dimensions which lie beyond the domain of technology. It is this unavoidable responsibility of the agronomists which establishes them as educators and makes them (among others) agents of change. This means that their participation in the system of relationships between the peasants, nature, and culture cannot be reduced to a *being before,* or a *being over,* or a *being for* the peasants, but a *being with* them in that they also are subjects of change.

This responsibility is not exclusively that of the agronomist-educator, nor even of educators in general, but of all those who in one way or another contribute to the impact of agrarian reform. Like the process of structural change, this process cannot be interpreted as a mechanical one, outside of time, which does not require the participation of human beings. Agrarian reform is not a purely technical matter. It involves political decisions that give effect and impulse to the technological proposals which, in that they are not neutral, affirm the ideological positions of the technologists. New technology (to deal with this aspect only) can thus either support or negate the active participation of the peasants as truly co-responsible elements in the process of change. Technology can, however, offer mechanistic solutions which, when applied within a human frame of reference (and agrarian reform is clearly within this domain) will be at most apparent successes if not objective failures. "It is not technical methods but the association of man and his tools which transforms a society."[21]

In the process of agrarian reform, there should be no exclusive support for either "technology" or for "humanity " Any program of agrarian reform which regards these two terms as antagonistic is naïve, whether it is the attitude superficially termed "humanist" (at heart reactionary, traditionalist and anti-transformation) which denies techniques, or whether it is the myth of techniques which in turn implies a dehumanization, a kind of messianism of techniques, conferring on technology the role of an infallible saviour. This messianism nearly always ends up by instigating the kind of programs in which humans are diminished in stature. Technical messianism (which is bourgeois in character) proposes modernization of existing structures in opposition to traditionalism, which seeks to maintain the status quo. According to this messianic conception, the passing from the old structures to the new "modernized" structures is as mechanical as the transportation of a chair from one place to another.

Since this mechanical attitude attempts to identify its modernizing action with development, it is important that I distinguish between the two. Modernization of a purely mechanical, automatic, and manipulating type has the center of decision for change not in the area undergoing transformation but outside it. The society in transformation is

21. Octavio Paz: *Claude Levi-Strauss and the New Feast of Aesop,* Editorial Joaquin, Mortiz, Mexico, 1st edition 1957, p. 97.

not the subject of its own transformation. On the contrary, the point of decision in the process of development lies within the being undergoing transformation—the process is not a mechanical one. Hence, while all development is modernization, not all modernization is development.

Agrarian reform should be a process of development which will result in the modernization of the rural areas along with the modernization of agriculture. If this is how agrarian reform is seen, the modernization resulting from that reform will not be the product of an automatic passage from the old to the new. (Strictly speaking this would not be a "passage," but rather the superposition of the new on the old.) In the non-mechanical concept the new is born from the old through the creative transformation emerging from advanced technology *combined* with the empirical methods of the peasants. This means that it is impossible to ignore the cultural background which explains the technical-empirical methods of the peasants. It is on this cultural foundation—from which their forms of behavior and their perception of reality are comprised—that all those who have some responsibility for the process of agrarian reform must base their work.

It should be obvious that while the transformation of the structure of *latifundia,* together with the reform of land-tenure (followed by the application of new technology) is unquestionably a factor of change in the peasant perception, this does not mean that one can dispense with action on the cultural plane. As a general process agrarian reform cannot be limited to unilateral actions in the sphere of production—commercialization, techniques, etc. It should rather unite such efforts to other equally necessary forms of action: deliberate, systematized, planned, cultural transformation. Hence, in agrarian reform in Chile the "settlement,"[22] precisely because it is a production-unit (I repeat that production does not exist without the man/woman-world relationship), should

---

22. *asentamiento:* in Chile the name given to a landholding expropriated by the government.

also be a pedagogical unit, in the broad sense of the term This pedagogical unit is one in which the educators are not only those who happen to work with what is usually termed education but are also agronomists, administrators, planners, researchers, peasants—in fact all those who have some connection with the process.

It is imperative that we protect ourselves from a mechanistic notion of reform. Such a naïve, narrow outlook tends to scorn the basic contribution of other sectors of knowledge. It tends towards rigidity and bureaucracy. To speak to a technocrat of the need for sociologists, social psychologists, or educators in the process of agrarian reform produces a hint of mistrust. Therefore to speak of the need for study in the field of philosophical anthropology and linguistics constitutes a scandal to be suppressed. In fact all these are of fundamental importance for the success which agrarian reform expects to achieve. For example, what would technocrats say if we spoke of the value of a linguistic investigation of the semantic universe of the areas undergoing reform (and of the areas outside the effects of reform)? They could not understand that such an investigation could make it possible for us to discover a series of aspects which are fundamental to their own action in the domain of technical methods. From the extension of peasant vocabulary to the analysis of the "pragmatic" content of the terms, to the study of its "associative field of meaning," one arrives at possible significant "themes," referred to in the "associative field of meaning" of those terms. However, technocrats would never understand the unquestionable contribution of present studies in "structural anthropology," in linguistics or of semantics to agrarian reform. For a technocrat all this is wasting time. It is the dreams of idealists and of those without a sense of the practical.

The technocrats would also think in this way if, following the same line of thought, they were approached about study and research on the different levels of the peasant consciousness. Such consciousness is conditioned by the structure in which this consciousness is developed through historical and existential experience, and therefore could provide critical information for the developing of reform programs. However technocrats would be unable to understand the "remaining behind" in the transformed structure of the "mythical aspects" forming part of the old structure. It is sufficient for them as orthodox technocrats for the structure to be transformed in such a way that everything that made up the former structure is eliminated. When, failing to recognize the people as cultural beings, they do not achieve the results they were expecting from their unilaterally technical action, they seek an explanation for their failure—and always find it "in the natural incapacity of the peasants." Their error is to fail to recognize that the time in which generations live, experience, work, and die is not calendar time. It is a "real" time, or "duration," as Bergson calls it. Thus it is a time made up of events in which the peasants build up through the generations their way of being (or *state of being*) which carries over into the new structure. This is why when the time in agrarian reform—a new time —is generated from the old time, the old co-exists with the new. The peasants in the "new time" thus manifest in their behavior the same duality which they had under the structure of *latifundia*. This is completely normal. "Human beings are not just what they are, but also what they were";[23] they are in a *state of being*, this being a characteristic of human existence. Human existence, therefore, contrary to animal or vegetable life, is a *process* taking place in one's own time.

There exists, then, a solid link between the present and the past, within which the present points towards the future, all within the framework of historical continuity. Thus it is that there are no rigid boundaries in time, whose "epochal" units interpenetrate one another. In order to understand this I shall make use of two concepts developed

---

23. This sentence is in quotation because of its resemblance to the following: "Mind is in all its manifestations not only what it is, but what it was," Zevede Barbu: *Problems of Historical Psychology*.

by Eduardo Nicol[24] when he discusses the question of historical truth which cannot be apprehended without historical continuity. These concepts are: "vertical structure" and "horizontal structure." "Vertical structure" forms the framework of the transformation of relationships between human beings and the world. It is with the products of this transformation that human beings create their world—the world of culture which is prolonged into the world of history. The sphere of culture and history, the human sphere of "vertical structure," is characterized by intersubjectivity and intercommunication. But if intercommunication existed only within a single "epochal" unit, there would be no historical continuity. This can be explained in that intersubjectivity and intercommunication pass through one "epochal" unit, and continue through to the next. This intercommunicating solidarity between different "epochal" units constitutes the field of "horizontal structure."

If this is valid from the viewpoint of understanding science and "logos" (which is the point of arrival of an "epochal" unit in horizontal relation to the "logos" or the science of another unit), it is also valid for the understanding of the forms of being and knowing in the domain of "doxa" from one "epochal" unit to another. It is therefore impossible to overlook solidarity between the "vertical structure" (in Nicol's sense) of the period of *latifundia* and the new structure of the "settlements." This solidarity emerges in the "horizontal structure." This being so, it is imperative that all those who work with the process of agrarian reform take into account the basic characteristics of peasant life in the reality of the *latifundia*. Only the naïveté of a technocrat could permit the belief that once agrarian reform is planned and put into practice everything that existed previously ceases to exist; that reform constitutes the rigid dividing line between the old and the new.

Agrarian reform seen critically is, in fact, an all-encom-

---

24. Eduardo Nicol: *The Principles of Science,* Fondo de Cultura Económica, Mexico, 1965.

passing action which is carried out within a totality—the reality which is to be transformed. This does not mean that the new emerging reality remains uninfluenced by the former reality. Hence, in reply to the challenges raised by the actual process of agrarian reform, the critical vision of the process reveals great possibilities for the use of specialized staff for specific jobs, without lapsing into "specialties." The technical training of specialists for work mainly in the area of technology goes hand-in-hand with serious reflections, studies, and analyses of the wider dimensions of which technology is only one part. A critical attitude towards agrarian reform, with an emphasis on cultural change which recognizes the need for a perceptual change,[25] opens up a new and fertile field of work for the agronomist-educator. Inspired by a critical vision of agrarian reform, the agronomists should concentrate on something more than mere technical aid. As agents of change, together *with* the peasants (who themselves are agents) it is incumbent on them to enter into the process of transformation, conscientizing both peasants and themselves at the same time. The conscientization I shall discuss in the final part of this work is an inter-conscientization.

While the naïve technocratic conception of agrarian reform does not take into account the fact that features which characterized the old structure remain in the new one, (thinking that problems are solved by technical "training"[26]) the critical vision of the process, without forgetting questions of technical instruction, places these within a broader framework. This professional instruction is not, for the critical mind, the naïve act of transferring or "depositing" technology. It is the act by which the technical process is offered to the educatee as a problem which must be solved. The critical conception of agrarian reform (in which there

25. Paulo Freire: *The Role of the Social Worker in the Process of Transformation. op. cit.*
26. The critical conception of the process does not use the term "training" with reference to people. "Trees are *cultivated,* animals are *trained,* people are *educated*"—says Kant.

is ready awareness of the significance of "vertical structure" as the cultural and historical world in which perception is formed) puts its maximum effort in the direction of the transformation of perception. Because this conception is a critical one, it is aware that the transformation of perception is not brought about at a purely intellectual level, but with the aid of a genuine praxis which requires a constant action on reality, and a reflection on this action. This implies a sound manner of *thinking* and *acting*. Hence, as I have suggested, large-scale, intensive cultural spade-work is absolutely indispensable for this conception.

Cultural transformation, which will continue to advance inexorably with the transformation of the reality of the *latifundium* and which will lead to a new "vertical structure," requires action in the field of "popular culture." This will produce direct intervention in the sphere of perception and will help to accelerate cultural transformation. In the process of agrarian reform, this then is the basic task of the agronomist: rather than being a removed and distant technocrat, s/he is an educator who is involved, who goes into the process of transformation *with* the peasants, as a Subject *with* other Subjects.

Chapter III

a) EXTENSION OR COMMUNICATION?

From the first pages of this essay I have insisted that humans, as beings of relationships, are challenged by nature, which they transform through their work. The result of this transformation, which separates itself off from them, is their world. This is the world of culture which is prolonged into the world of history. This exclusive world of human beings with which geographical space is filled Eduardo Nicol describes (as I pointed out in the previous chapter) as a world of "vertical structure," related to a "horizontal structure." The "vertical structure," the social, human world would not exist if it were not a world able to communicate. Without communication human knowledge could not be propagated.

Intersubjectivity, or intercommunication, is the primordial characteristic of this cultural and historical world. The gnosiological function cannot be reduced to a simple relation between a Subject that knows and a knowable object. Without a relation of communication between Subjects that know, with reference to a knowable object, the act of knowing would disappear. The gnosiological relationship does not therefore find its term in the object known. Communication between Subjects about the object is established by means of intersubjectivity. This is why Eduardo Nicol[1] after studying the three relationships comprising knowledge—the gnosiological, the logical, and the historical—adds a fourth one, which is fundamental and indispensable to the act of knowing—the relationship of dialogue. Just as there is no such thing as an isolated human being there is also no such thing as isolated thinking. Any act of thinking requires a Subject who thinks, an object thought about which mediates the thinking Subjects, and the communication between the lat-

---

1. Eduardo Nicol: *op. cit.*

ter, manifested by linguistic signs. Thus the world of human beings is a world of communication. As a conscious being (whose consciousness is one of intentionality towards the world and towards reality), the human being acts, thinks, and speaks on and about this reality, which is the mediation between him or her and other human beings who also act, think, and speak.

Discussing the function of thought, Nicol[2] affirms that it should not be designated by a noun, but by a *transitive* verb. Strictly speaking, one could perhaps say that the verb designating thought should not be merely transitive, but should take (syntactically) the object of the action *and* an *accompanying complement*. In addition to the thinking Subject and the object thought about, the presence of another thinking Subject would be necessary (just as necessary as that of the first Subject and object), which would figure in the accompanying expression. This would take the form of a "co-subjective-objective" verb, whose action on the *object* would be one of "co-participation."

The thinking Subject cannot think alone. In the act of thinking about the object s/he cannot think without the co-participation of another Subject. There is no longer an "I think" but "we think." It is the "we think" which establishes the "I think" and not the contrary. This co-participation of the Subjects in the act of thinking is communication. Thus the object is not the end of the act of thinking, but the mediator of communication. Hence it cannot be *communicated* from one Subject to another as the object of communication, i.e., a communiqué. If the object of thought were a mere *communiqué*, it would not be a significant meaning, mediating the Subjects. However, once the object provides, through communication, the mediation between two Subjects "A" and "B," the subject "A" cannot have the object as an exclusive term of thought. Neither can "A" transform the Subject "B" into a depository for his thinking. When this does occur there is no communication. It

---

2. Eduardo Nicol: *op. cit.*

means only that one Subject is transforming another into a recipient of his communiqués.[3]

Communication implies a reciprocity which cannot be broken. Hence it is not possible to comprehend thought without its double function, as something which learns and as something which communicates. But this function is not the *extension* of the significant content of the object (i.e., the object of knowing and thinking). To communicate is to communicate about the significant content of the object. Thus during communication there are no passive Subjects. Subjects showing co-intentionality towards the object of their thought communicate its content to each other. Communication is characterized by the fact that it is dialogue, in that dialogue communicates.

In the relationship between communication and dialogue the Subjects engaged in dialogue express themselves through a system of linguistic signs. For the act of communication to be successful, there must be accord between the reciprocally communicating Subjects. That is, the verbal expression of one of the Subjects must be perceptible within a frame of reference that is meaningful to the other Subject. If this agreement on the linguistic signs used to express the object signified does not exist, there can be no comprehension between the Subjects, and communication will be impossible. The truth of this can be seen in that there is no separation between comprehension (intelligibility) and communication, as if the two comprised different moments of the same process or the same act. On the contrary, intelligibility and communication occur simultaneously. Whether or not we pay serious attention to our relations with the peasants (however they may concern us) will depend on whether we are aware of this particular observation. In dealing with a fact such as a harvest, for example, we could use a system of symbols which would not be intelligible to peasants. They

---

3. In this sense the communiqués are the "meanings" which in losing their own dynamism turn into static, crystallized contents. These contents are deposited by one Subject in others thereby preventing the process of thinking. This is typical behavior of the "educator" in what I ironically term the "banking" concept of education.

could fail to understand our technical jargon with its own
universe of linguistic signs. (Which suggests that normal
classroom techniques are less and less recommendable for
efficiency.) Problem-posing dialogue, in addition to the various reasons already mentioned which make it indispensable,
diminishes the difference between the sense of an expression
as given by a technician, and the grasping of this expression
by the peasants in terms of its meaning for them. Thus the
sense of the expression comes to signify the same for both.
This occurs only in the communication and intercommunication of thinking Subjects. It never occurs in the *extension* of
what is thought from one Subject to another.

It is not superfluous to emphasize the need for serious
semantic studies which should be indispensable to the work
of the agronomist. What is intelligible is only communicated
insofar as it is communicable. This is why, when the significant content of the object under discussion is not compre-
hensible to one of the Subjects, communication cannot take
place. In such cases both interlocutor-Subjects have to seek
such comprehension through dialogue. For although one of
them has achieved this understanding it cannot be grasped
by the other as it is being expressed by the first. It is thus
obvious that a search for knowledge which is reduced to the
simple relationship knowing Subject-knowable object (thus
destroying the dialogical structure of knowledge) is a mistaken one, however much it may be a tradition.

Equally mistaken is the conception which sees the task of
education as an act of transmission or as the systematic extension of knowledge. On the contrary, instead of being the
transference of knowledge—which more or less "kills"
knowledge—education is the gnosiological condition in its
broadest sense. The educator's task is not that of one who
sets himself or herself as a knowing Subject before a knowable object, and, having come to know it, proceeds to discourse on it to the educatees, whose role it is to file away the
"communiqués." Education is communication and dialogue.[4]
It is not the transference of knowledge, but the encounter

---

4. Discussed more fully in the second part of this chapter.

of Subjects in dialogue in search of the significance of the object of knowing and thinking.

To illustrate this analysis of communication it is helpful to examine how Urban[5] classifies acts of communication. According to him, these acts occur basically on two levels. On one level the object of communication belongs to the sphere of emotion. On another level knowledge is communicated. In the first case (which is of no concern in this essay) communication manifested on an emotive level "operates by contagion."[6] In this type of communication one of the Subjects evokes a certain emotional state in another (fear, joy, hate, etc.), and can be influenced by this state. Alternatively s/he can get to know this state in the Subject manifesting it. However, in this kind of communication, which is also found at an animal level, there is no "entering into" the object by the communicating Subjects.[7]

The "entering into" the object of communication, expressed by linguistic signs, is the second type of communication distinguished by Urban. Here communication operates between Subjects about something which mediates them and which is "offered" to them as a knowable fact. This something which mediates the interlocutor-Subjects can be a concrete fact (sowing and the techniques of sowing, for example), or a mathematical theorem. In both these cases true communication is not, in my opinion, the exclusive transfer or transmission of knowledge from one Subject to another, but rather his co-participation in the act of comprehending the object. It is communication carried out in a critical way. On an emotive level communication can take place both be-

---

5. Quoted by Adam Schaff: *Introduction to Semantics*, Fondo de Cultura Economica, Mexico, 1966, p. 128.
6. *Op. cit.*, p. 129.
7. The strongly emotional character of the communication prevents the Subject expressing it from standing back from himself and from his situation so that he can see himself, "see it" and "contemplate it." The same operation is also made difficult for his interlocutor, who in one way or another finds himself caught up in the emotional situation. Thus it is difficult for either of them to have in the *state expressed* the object about which they intercommunicate at the level of knowledge.

tween Subject "A" and Subject "B," and between a crowd and a charismatic leader. Its main characteristic is to be a-critical. In the prior case communication implies the comprehension by intercommunicating Subjects of the content with reference to which the relationship of communication is established. As I emphasized in the first pages of this chapter, communication on this level is essentially linguistic.

This fact raises important problems which cannot be forgotten or lightly dealt with. They can be reduced to the following: Efficient communication requires the Subjects in dialogue to direct their "entering into" towards the same object. It requires that they express it by means of linguistic signs belonging to a linguistic universe common to both so that they can have a similar comprehension of the object of communication. In this communication, which operates through words, the relation *thought-language-context or reality* cannot be broken. There is no thought which does not have some reference to reality and which is not directly or indirectly influenced by reality. Hence the language expressing this thought cannot fail to show this influence too. The error to which the concept of extension can lead is clear. It is one of "extending" technical knowledge to the peasants, instead of making (by efficient communication) the concrete fact to which this knowledge refers (expressed by linguistic signs) the object of the mutual comprehension of peasants and agronomist alike. It is only with the co-participation of the peasants that communication can work efficiently, and only by means of this communication can agronomists successfully carry out their work.

Let us now look at another problem of equal importance in the field of communication, which agronomist-educators must take into consideration in their work. As I have already said, there can be no communication, if the comprehension of the meaning (signification) of the sign is not established among the Subjects-in-dialogue.[8] If the sign does

---

8. Misunderstandings are common between Brazilians newly arrived in Chile and native Chileans. The similarity of linguistic signs from an ortho-

not have the same meaning (signification) for the Subjects in communication, communication ceases to be viable for lack of an indispensable comprehension. On this aspect Adam Schaff[9] differentiates two types of communication: one concerned with *significata,* the other whose content is made up of *convictions.* In communication when the content is comprised of convictions, there is not only the question of the meaningful comprehension of the signs, but also the question of adhesion or non-adhesion to the conviction expressed by one of the communicating Subjects. For *meaningful* comprehension of the signs, the communicating Subjects must be able to reconstitute within themselves the dynamic process from which the conviction they express by means of the linguistic signs is developed.

I am able to understand the signification of the linguistic signs of a peasant from the Northeast of Brazil who tells me, with absolute conviction, that he cures the infected wounds of his animals by praying over the tracks they leave in the mud. As was stated above, to understand the signification of the linguistic signs used by the peasant implies that we comprehend the context in which the conviction expressed by those signs was engendered. However, neither the comprehension of the signs nor the comprehension of the context are sufficient to make me share his conviction. Thus, in not sharing the conviction or the magic belief of this peasant, I invalidate all that it contains in the way of "theory" or pseudo-science, which includes a whole area of "technical knowledge." What cannot be ignored is that contrary to the magic belief of the peasant, the domain of accepted meanings (in the sense examined here and by Schaff), seems to the peasant to be a contradiction of his "science." The

---

graphic and sometimes a prosodic point of view does not extend to their meaning. For a Brazilian woman in day-to-day language *botar la mesa* (in Portuguese: *botar a mesa*) means to serve a meal at table; for a Chilean woman it means to throw or knock the table to the ground. If you say to a Chilean child newly arrived in Brazil, "Son, you can take the book" (in Spanish: *Mi hijo, puedes tirar el libro*), he will very probably throw it down or throw it away.

9. Adam Schaff: *op. cit.* p. 164

magic conviction of the peasant, a conviction related to his incipient empirical methods, naturally comes into conflict with the technical "significata" of the agronomists. Thus it is that the relation between agronomist and peasants, planned and systematic as it is, must still unfold within a dialogical, communicating, gnosiological setting.

Even if I agreed—and this is not the case—with the "extension" form of the act of knowing, in which one subject takes the knowledge to another (who thus ceases to be a Subject), it would not only be necessary that the signs should have the same meaning, but also that the content of the knowledge "extended" should have something in common with both poles of the relationship. As this is not the case, extension has the tendency to use the methods of propaganda and persuasion in the vast area which goes by the name of "mass-media communication." These methods constitute a means of issuing *communiquées* to the masses. Through such methods the masses are directed and manipulated, and because of this do not become involved in the process of education for liberation. My comments are directed at those who make use of such means by error, and not for other reasons. One of the reasons for the error is that, when agronomists encounter the first difficulties in their attempt to communicate with the peasants, they do not realize that they are caused by the fact (among others) that the process of communication between human beings cannot ignore totally socio-cultural conditioning. Instead of taking their own conditioning as well as that of the peasants into account they simplify the question and conclude (as was stated in a previous chapter) that the peasants are incapable of dialogue. From this point to acts of cultural invasion and manipulation is only a step, which has practically been taken.

There is another thing which should be considered very important in the process of communication for the work of educators in their relationships with the peasants. We refer here to certain manifestations occurring in the process of communication, which are either natural or socio-cultural.

Both function within the social relationships of communication as signs which indicate or announce something. The cause-and-effect relationship which the peasants are able to perceive between these signs—natural or not—and certain facts, is not always the same as that which the agronomists perceive. In either case, whether the indicators are natural or socio-cultural, the communication between agronomists and peasants can be interrupted if the agronomists inadvertently take up positions which could be considered negative within the set limits of any one of these indicators.

Some final considerations are indispensable to this chapter, namely on the humanist aspect which should inspire the work of communication between technicians and peasants in the process of agrarian reform. This humanist aspect is not abstract. It is concrete and rigorously scientific. This humanism is not based on visions of an ideal human being, separated from the world, the portrait of an imaginary person, however well-intentioned the person imagining might be. This humanism does not try to concretize a timeless model, a sort of idea or myth, for in this way humans become alienated. This humanism does not claim to be a *what will be* for lack of a critical vision of concrete human beings who tragically are in a *state of being* which is almost *not being*. This humanism on the contrary, is based on science, and not on "doxa." Not on "I should like it to be so," nor on purely humanitarian gestures. It is a humanism concerned with the humanization of men and women, rejecting all forms of manipulation as the contradiction of liberation. This humanism which sees men and women in the world and in time, "mixed in" with reality, is only true humanism when it engages in action to transform the structures in which they are reified. This humanism refuses both despair and naïve optimism, and is thus hopefully critical. Its critical hope rests on an equally critical belief, the belief that human beings can make and remake things, that they can transform the world. A belief then that human beings, by making and remaking things and transforming the world, can transcend the situation in which their *state of being* is almost a *state of non-being*, and go on to a *state of being*, in search of *becoming more* fully human. This scientific humanism (which cannot fail to be loving) must be aided by the action through communication of the agronomist-educator.

Once more I am obliged to deny the term extension the connotations of a truly educational practice as it exists in the concept of communication. I would therefore answer the question asked not only in the title of this chapter but in the whole essay—"extension or communication?"—negatively with regard to extension and positively with regard to communication.

b) EDUCATION AS A GNOSIOLOGICAL STATE

The human being is a conscious body. His or ner consciousness, with its "intentionality" towards the world, is always consciousness *of* something. It is in a permanent state of moving towards reality. Hence the condition of the human being is to be in constant relationship to the world. In this relationship subjectivity, which takes its form in objectivity, combines with the latter to form a dialectical unity from which emerges knowledge closely linked with action. This is why unilaterally subjective and objective explanations which sever this dialectic are unable to comprehend reality. If an erroneous solipsism claims that only the Ego exists and that its consciousness embraces everything (since it is an absurdity to think of a reality external to it), the a-critical, mechanistic, grossly materialistic objectivism, according to which reality transforms itself, without any action on the part of men and women (who are mere objects of transformation)[1] is equally in error.

These two erroneous ways of considering human beings and of explaining their presence in the world and their role in history also engender false conceptions of education. One starts by denying all concrete, objective reality and declares that the consciousness is the exclusive creator of its own concrete reality. The other denies the presence of human beings as transforming beings in the world, and subordinates them to the transformation of reality which takes place without their involvement. Idealism errs in affirming that ideas which are separate from reality govern the historical process. So does the mechanistic objectivism which transforms human beings into abstractions and denies them

---

1. In his Third Thesis on Feuerbach, Marx says: "The materialist theory that men are the product of circumstances and of education, and that, therefore modified men are the product of different circumstances and a different education, forgets that the circumstances are actually transformed by men, and that the educator himself needs to be educated." Marx-Engels, *Selected Works* Moscow, 1966. Thesis on Feuerbach III, pp. 404–405.

their presence as beings of decision in historical transformations.

Education based on one or the other of these forms of
negating human beings leads to nothing. Human beings must
be seen in their interaction with reality which they feel and
perceive, and on which they exercise the process of transformation. It is in its dialectical relations with reality that I
shall discuss education as a constant process for the liberation of human beings. Education cannot view men and
women isolated from the world (creating it in their consciousness) nor the world without men and women (incapable of transforming it). Education would become a-histori-
cal in the first case for lack of the world, in the second case,
because men and women would be excluded. History cannot
exist without both of these. One does not find only a mechanistic process in which human beings are merely incidental
to facts. Nor does one find the result of the ideas of a few
human beings which have been developed in their consciousness. History, as a period of human events, is made by human beings at the same time as they "make" themselves in
history. If the work of education, like any other human
undertaking, cannot operate other than "within" the world
of human beings (which is a historical-cultural world), the
relations between human beings and the world must constitute the starting-point for our reflections on that undertaking. These relations do not constitute a mere enunciation, a
simple sentence. They involve a dialectical situation in
which one of the poles is the person and the other the objective world—a world in creation, as it were. If this historical-cultural world were a created, finished world, it
would no longer be susceptible to transformation. The human being exists as such, and the world is a historical-cultural one, because the two come together as unfinished products in a permanent relationship, in which human beings
transform the world and undergo the effects of their transformation. In this dynamic, historical-cultural process, one
generation encounters the objective reality marked out by

another generation and receives through it the imprints of reality.

Any attempt to manipulate people to adapt them to this reality (quite apart from being scientifically absurd, since adaptation implies the existence of a finished, static reality —not one which is being created) means taking from them their opportunity and their right to transform the world. Education cannot take this road. To be authentic it must be liberating. One of its basic preoccupations must be the greater penetration of the "prise de conscience" which operates in human beings when they act and when they work. This deepening of the *prise de conscience* which takes place through conscientization, is not and never can be an intellectual or an individualistic effort. Conscientization cannot be arrived at by a psychological, idealist subjectivist road, nor through objectivism, for all the reasons I have mentioned. Just as the *prise de conscience* cannot operate in isolated individuals, but through the relations of transformation they establish between themselves and the world, so also conscientization can only operate in this way. The *prise de conscience,* which is a human characteristic, results as we have seen, in a person's coming face to face with the world and with concrete reality, which is presented as a process of objectification. Any objectification implies a perception which is conditioned by the elements of its own reality. The *prise de conscience* exists on different levels. There is a magic level as well as a level in which the objectified fact fails to be apprehended in all its complexity.

If the *prise de conscience* goes beyond the mere *apprehension* of the presence of a fact, and places it critically in the system of relationships within the totality in which it exists, it transcends itself, deepens, and becomes conscientization. This effort of the *prise de conscience* to transcend itself and achieve conscientization, which always requires one's critical insertion in the reality which one begins to unveil, cannot, I must repeat, be individual but social. It is sufficient to know that conscientization does not take place in abstract beings in the air but in real men and women and in social structures, to understand that it cannot remain on the level of the individual. It would not be superfluous to repeat that conscientization, which can only be manifested in the concrete praxis (which can never be limited to the mere activity of the consciousness) is never neutral; in the same way, education can never be neutral. Those who talk of neutrality are precisely those who are afraid of losing their right to use neutrality to their own advantage. In the conscientization process the educator has the right, as a person, to have options. What s/he does not have is the right to impose them. To do this is to prescribe these options for others. To prescribe is to manipulate. To manipulate is "to reify" and to reify is to establish a relationship of "domestication" which may be disguised behind an apparently inoffensive façade. In this case, it is impossible to speak of conscientization. The false educator can only "domesticate" because instead of undertaking the critical task of demythifying reality, s/he mythifies it further. It is indispensable for such educators to issue *communiquées* instead of communicating and receiving communications. At no moment can they establish a truly gnosiological relationship since this would make manipulation impossible.

This then is why I say that "education as the practice of freedom" is not the transfer, or transmission of knowledge or cultures. Nor is it the extension of technical knowledge. It is not the act of depositing reports or facts in the educatee. It is not the "perpetuation of the values of a given culture." It is not "an attempt to adapt the educatee to the milieu."

I see "education as the practice of freedom" above all as a truly gnosiological situation. In this the act of knowing does not have its term in the knowable object since it is communicated to other Subjects which are also capable of knowing. In the educational process for liberation, educator-educatee and educatee-educator are both cognitive Subjects before knowable objects which mediate them. One can say then, and I have heard it on numerous occasions: "How can educator and educatee possibly be put on a par in the search for knowledge if it is the former who already knows? How can the educatee be said to be capable of knowing if his or her role is to learn from the educator?" These observations, which are basically objections, cannot conceal the preconceptions of the person who makes them. They always originate with those who consider themselves to be the possessors of wisdom face to face with the educatees who are regarded as ignorant. Education through dialogue and communication is seen by them in their misinterpretation (whether erroneous or ideological) as a threat. It is in fact a threat to their false knowledge.

Many of those who reject communication, and avoid the true state of knowing which is a state of participation *with*, do so because in the face of knowable objects, they are incapable of taking up a cognitive position. They remain in the realm of "doxa" beyond which they are the mere repeaters of texts read but not known. In truly gnosiological education there is not one particular moment in which, all alone in a library or laboratory, the educator "knows," and another moment in which s/he simply narrates, discourses on, or explains the knowledge "received." At the moment in which educators carry out their research, when as cognitive Subjects they stand face to face with a knowable object, they are only apparently alone. Not only do they establish a mysterious, invisible dialogue with those who carried out the same act of knowing before them, but they engage in a dialogue with themselves too. Place face to face before themselves they investigate and question themselves. The more they ask questions the more they feel that their curiosity about the object of their knowledge is not decreasing. It only diminishes if it is isolated from human beings and the world.

This is why dialogue as a fundamental part of the structure of knowledge needs to be opened to other Subjects in the knowing process. Thus the class is not a class in the traditional sense, but a meeting-place where knowledge is sought and not where it is transmitted. Just because the edu cator's task is not dichotomized into two separate moments (one in which s/he "knows," and another in which s/he speaks about this "knowledge"), education is a permanent act of cognition. Educators never allow themselves to be bureaucratized by high-sounding, repetitious, mechanical explanations. So much so that whenever an educatee asks a question, educators in their explanations remake the whole previous effort of cognition. Remaking the effort does not, however, mean repeating it as it was. It means making a new effort, in a new situation, in which new aspects which were not clear before are clearly presented to the educatee. New ways of access to the object are opened to him or her.

The teachers who do not make this effort, because they merely memorize their lessons, must of necessity reject education as a gnosiological condition and can thus have no love for the dialogue of communication. Education for them is the transfer of "knowledge." It consists in extending this "knowledge" to passive educatees and preventing them from experiencing the development of the active, participatory condition, characteristic of someone who knows. This false conception of education, based on the depositing of "reports" in the educatees, is a basic obstacle to transformation. It is an anti-historical conception of education. Educational systems based on this conception surround themselves with a "barricade" which inhibits creativity. For creativity does not develop within an empty formalism, but within the praxis of human beings with each other in the world and with the world. In this praxis action and reflection constantly and mutually illuminate each other. Its practice, which involves a theory from which it is inseparable, also implies the attitude of someone seeking knowledge, and not someone passively receiving it. Thus, when education is not a truly gnosiological condition, it diminishes into a verbalism which, because it frustrates, is not inconsequential.

The relations between verbalist educators, who discourse on memorized "knowledge" (which has not been researched or carefully examined) and their educatees is a type of edu cational technical aid. In this type of technical aid empty words are like the "presents" characteristic of forms of aid in the social field. Both forms of technical aid—material or intellectual—prevent those "aided" from having a clear and critical view of reality. Such aid prevents them from "unveiling," from revealing and apprehending reality as it is. It prevents those "aided" from seeing themselves as being "aided."[2] When education abandons the true gnosiological condition to take the form of verbal narrative, it deprives the educatees of the chance of transcending the domain of "doxa" and reaching that of "logos." If they succeed in this, it is in spite of their education.

The "technical aid" conception of education "anaesthetizes" the educatees and leaves them a-critical and naïve in the face of the world. But the conception of education which recognizes (and lives in this recognition) that it is a gnosiological condition, challenges them to think rather than to memorize. The former is rigid, dogmatic, and authoritarian. The latter is mobile and critical. It does not confound authority with authoritarianism, nor liberty with libertinism. It recognizes within time the relations between one epochal unit and another which builds across the "horizontal structure" and explains cultural "duration." "Duration" does not mean *permanence* but the interplay between permanence and transformation.[3] In the first conception education is an instrument of domination. In the second it is the constant search for liberation.

If education is the relation between Subjects in the knowing process mediated by the knowable object, in which the

---

2. However, the fact that aid, whatever its form, contains this obstructive feature, does not mean that those receiving aid cannot emerge sooner or later from their condition of being aided in order to establish themselves as beings of decision by action. I venture to state that the movements of rebellion which are prevalent today have a lot to do with the emergence of the young (and in certain areas the people) who break with a "technically aided" and "technically aiding" world. They place in question the validity of the "communiqués" issued in the name of "technical aid" on the subject of human existence. Their preoccupations concern not only the instrumental field of *how,* but extend to the *what, why,* and *wherefore* of things in the field of action and existence.

3. See Paulo Freire: "*The Role of the Social Worker in the Process of Transformation,*" op. cit.

educator permanently reconstructs the act of knowing, it must then be problem-posing. The task of the educator is to present to the educatees as a problem the content which mediates them, and not to discourse on it, give it, extend it, or hand it over, as if it were a matter of something already done, constituted, completed, and finished. In the act of problematizing the educatees, the educator is problematized too. Problematization is so much a dialectic process that it would be impossible for anyone to begin it without becoming involved in it. No one can present something to someone else as a problem and at the same time remain a mere spectator of the process. S/he will be problematized even if methodologically speaking, s/he prefers to remain silent after posing the problem, while the educatees capture, analyze, and comprehend it.

In the process of problematization, any step made by a Subject to penetrate the problem-situation continually opens up new roads for other Subjects to comprehend the object being analyzed. Educators who are problematized by engaging in this kind of action "re-enter into" the object of the problem through the "entering into" of the educatees. This is why educators continue to learn. The humbler they are in this process the more they will learn. Problematization takes place in the field of communication and concerns real, concrete, existential situations. Or it concerns intellectual contents again linked to the concrete. It requires that the interlocutor-Subjects, who have been problematized, understand the total meaning of the signs (linguistic and otherwise) used in communication. The understanding of the signs comes from the dialogue, which makes possible the exact understanding of the terms with which the Subjects express the critical analysis of the problem in which they are involved. I should once again emphasize that problematization is not an intellectual diversion, both alienated and alienating. Nor is it an escape from action, a way of disguising the fact that what is real has been denied. Problematization is not only inseparable from the act of knowing but also inseparable from concrete situations.

Taking these last as the point of departure, an analysis of

concrete situations brings the Subjects once more to see themselves in their confrontation with such situations and to undergo again this confrontation. Thus problematization implies a critical return to action. It starts from action and returns to it. The process of problematization is basically someone's reflection on a content which results from an act, or reflection on the act itself in order to act better together with others within the framework of reality. There can be no problematization without reality. Discussion about *transcendence* must take its point of departure from discussion on the *here,* which for humans is always a *now* too.

The conception of education which I am defending, and which I present in summary as a problem-content to readers of this essay, centers around the problematization of the human being and the world, not the problematization of the human being isolated from the world, nor the world isolated from the human being. The relations created between them cannot be dichotomized. However, as this observation is important, it needs clarification. What *is* the problematization of the human being and the world? What *is* the problematization of the relations between them which cannot be dichotomized? This is not the problematization of the term "relation" *per se.* The term "relation" suggests the position of a human being face to face with the world, suggests that s/he is in it and with it as a being who works, acts, and transforms the world. It would be legitimate to discuss the concept of "relation" at the strictly human level, contrasting it, for example, with *contact,* at the animal level. It would be equally possible to discuss it from a linguistic, philosophical, sociological, anthropological, etc., point of view.

Of fundamental importance to education as an authentically gnosiological condition is the problematization of the world of work, products, ideas, convictions, aspirations, myths, art, science, the world in short of culture and history which is the result of the relations between human beings and the world. To present this human world as a problem for human beings is to propose that they "enter into" it critically, taking the operation as a whole, their action, and that of others on it. It means "re-entering into" the world through the "entering into" of the previous understandings which may have been arrived at naïvely because reality was not examined as a whole. In "entering into" their own world, people become aware of their manner of acquiring knowledge and realize the need of knowing even more. In this lies the whole force of education in the gnosiological condition.

Men and women as Subjects in the knowing process (and not receivers of a "knowledge" which others donate to them or prescribe for them) progress towards the *raison d'être* of reality. Reality shows them progressively a world a challenge and possibilities; of determinism and liberty; of negation and affirmation of their humanity; of permanence and transformation; of value and valuelessness; of expectation, in the hopefulness of search; and of expectation without hope in a fatalist inaction. The more they review critically their past and present experiences in and with the world, which they can see more clearly now because they are reliving it, the more they realize that the world is not a *cul-de-sac* for men and women, an unalterable state which crushes them. They discover—or become predisposed to discover—that education is not solely and exclusively per manence or change in something. Education is "duration," because it results from the interplay of these two opposites in dialogue. Education shows "duration" in the contradiction of permanence and change. This is why it is possible to say that education is permament only in the sense of duration. In this case "permanent" does not mean the permanence of values, but the permanence of the *educational process,* which is the interplay between cultural permanence and change.

The above-mentioned dialectic—permanence/change—which makes the educational process "durable," interprets education as something which is in a *state of being,* and not something which *is.* Hence, its historical-sociological aspect. If education did not adapt to the rhythm of reality it would not "last," because it would not be in a *state of being*. Thus education can also be a force for transformation, because it "lasts" to the degree that it transforms itself. But its transformation must be the result of the transformations effected in the reality to which it applies. This is to say that the education of a society stops being in a *state of being* if it is determined by the transformations effected in another society on which it depends. If the education of a society does not exist in a concrete context, showing the influence of human beings and at the same time influencing them, it cannot advance the transformation of the reality of that society. Imported education, which is the manifestation of a form of being of an alienated culture, is something which is merely superimposed on the reality of the importing society. Hence this education which *is not* because it is *not being* in a dialectic relationship with its context, contains no force of transformation for reality. As we can see, education as a gnosiological condition which unites educator and educatee as Subjects in the process of knowing, opens for them innumerable and indispensable roads leading to their affirmation as beings of praxis.

It is thus that we see the work of agronomist-educators. In it they must seek to know reality through dialogue with the peasants, in order to more effectively transform it together with the peasants. I said that education as a gnosiological condition means the problematization of the content on which educator and educatee as Subjects in the process of knowing concentrate. The Subjects in the process of knowing, in their co-intentionality towards the object, penetrate it in search of its *raison d'être*. And the object, in revealing itself to the Subjects, appears to them within a structural system in which it is in direct or indirect relation with another object. The object (which can be a problem-situation) initially "entered into" as if it were an isolated whole, "gives itself up" to the Subjects in the process of knowing as a "sub-whole" which in turn forms part of a greater totality. Step by step the Subjects in the process of knowing advance towards the union of the parts which make up the whole. Thus, for example, sowing is taken critically as part of a larger reality-cum-process. It is in direct relation not only to other aspects of this reality-cum-process but also to natural and cultural phenomena. Thus sowing is associated with soil conditions, with meteorological conditions, with the set time for carrying it out, with the kind of seeds, and also with the techniques used, with the magic beliefs of the peasants, as well as with land-tenure. In a sense, any effort implies an effort towards totalization.

It is not possible to teach methods without problematizing the whole structure in which these methods will be used. No program of literacy-training can exist—as the naïve claim[4]—which is not connected with the work of human beings, their technical proficiency, their view of the world. Any education work, whether the educator is an agronomist or not, which only means discoursing, narrating, or speaking about *something,* instead of challenging the capacity of reflection and knowledge of the educatees about it, not only neutralizes this capacity for knowledge, but merely skirts the problems. The educator's action encourages "naïveté" rather than conscientization on the part of the educatees. Thus the authenticity of technical aid depends upon its becoming educational actions (in the sense I have defined it), transcending the procedures of purely technical "assistentialism."

In the course of this chapter I have suggested an aspect which is of the greatest importance for the education I am defending. Of the Subjects in the knowing process, who proposes the basic themes which are the object of the act of knowing? If education as a gnosiological condition has its core in the dialogue relationship, since without it the co-intentionality of the Subjects of the knowable object would disappear, when does this relationship begin? How is the curriculum of this kind of education organized? The answers to these questions are more or less implicit not only in

---

4. For this see Paulo Freire: "La Alfabetisacion de Adultos: la critica de su vision ingenua y la comprension de su vision critica," *op. cit.*

this chapter but in the main part of this essay. However, because they are only implicit, it is incumbent on me to clarify them.

If education can be defended as an eminently gnosiological condition (which is therefore dialogical) in which educator-educatee and educatee-educator are problematized and unite around a knowable object, it is obvious that the point of departure of the dialogue is the quest for a curriculum. Thus the problem-contents which will make up the curriculum on which the Subjects will carry out their gnosiological action cannot be chosen by one or the other of the dialogical poles in isolation. If it were so, and unfortunately this is how it is seen (usually that the choice of direction falls exclusively on the educator), the task of education would take a vertical, donating, "aiding" form[5] from the beginning.

If the task of drawing-up the technical-aid program falls exclusively on the agronomist—and the team s/he works with—without taking into account the peasant's critical perception of their reality, even if s/he is up-to-date with the most urgent problems in the rural area in which s/he is going to work, s/he will tend toward the cultural invasion I spoke of in the last chapter. I have already mentioned this in other parts of this essay, but I will repeat it, that frequently what constitutes a real problem for us is nothing of the sort for the peasant, and vice versa. It is equally frequent for the peasants, in spite of the magical background of their culture, to show considerable empirical knowledge about basic problems of agricultural techniques. In any case, if the dialectics of education and its gnosiological aspect are taken into consideration, it is impossible to dispense with a preliminary knowledge of the aspirations, the levels of perception, the view of the world which the educatees (in this case the peasants) have. With this knowledge as a starting-

---

5. This anti-dialogical way of organizing the problems (which are prolonged in the anti-dialogue of the educational activities engaged in) fails not just because it contains an ideology of domination—and this is not always perceived by the person who uses it—but also by the total absence of scientific discipline. I hope to clarify this in the following pages.

point, the educational curriculum can be organized to include a group of themes on which educator and educatee as Subjects in the knowing process can use their ability to know.

To know the peasants' manner of seeing the world which contains their "generative themes" (which, after being taken, studied, and placed in a scientific setting, are returned to the peasants in the form of problem themes) implies a search. This in turn requires a methodology which should be, in my opinion, dialogical, problem-posing and conscientizing.[6] Research into the "generative themes," and education as a gnosiological condition, are different stages of the same process. If one offers the peasants their own theme, so that in the act of knowing they can dialogue on it with the educator (whether an agronomist or not) it will "generate" other themes when at a later stage it is apprehended in its relationship with other related themes through the transformation undergone by the perception of reality.[7] Thus one passes from a stage which tends mainly towards the search for the "generative theme" to another whose tendency is mainly educational-gnosiological. At the same time as the comprehension of reality is being heightened through the act of knowing, a new theme is being sought out.

Thus the content of education springs from the peasants themselves and their relations with the world, and transforms and broadens itself as the world becomes revealed to them. The "research groups" are prolonged into "cultural discussion groups." These in turn require new educational contents of different standards which demand further thematic research. This state of dialectic[8] generates a dynamic which transcends the static character of the naïve conception of education, which is the mere "transmission" of

---

6. See *Pedagogy...*
7. For the transformation of perception and structural transformation see Paulo Freire: *The Role of the Social Worker in the Process of Transformation, op. cit.*
8. For this see José Luis Fiori: "Dialectic or Liberty: Two Dimensions of the Search for Themes," ICIRA, Santiago.

knowledge. Hence, action based on it is the complete opposite of the action which consists merely of the extension of the contents which have been selected by one of its poles.

Technical aid, which is indispensable in any sphere, is only valid when its curriculum which grows out of the search for "generative themes" of the people, goes beyond pure technical instruction. Technical proficiency capacitation is more than just instruction, because it is a search for knowledge, using the appropriate procedures. It can never be reduced to the level of training (in the way animals are trained), since technical proficiency capacitation only takes place in a human setting. Unlike animals, whose activity *is* themselves, human beings are capable of reflecting not only on themselves but on their activity, which is something separate from them, just as the product of their activity is separate from them. Technical aid, of which proficiency capacitation is a part, can only exist through praxis, if it is to be genuine. It exists in action and reflection and in the critical comprehension of the implications of method. Technical proficiency capacitation as distinct from the training of animals can never be dissociated from the existential conditions of the life of the peasants, from their cultural viewpoint or from their magic beliefs. It must begin at the level at which they *are,* and not at the level at which the agronomist reckons they should be. It is when they are challenged to think about how and why they *exist* in a certain way, to which their own type of techniques corresponds, and when they are challenged to reflect on why and how they can use this or that type of technique, that they are really genuinely capacitated.

There is another aspect which I must clarify. Given that we can count on various groups of peasants in a certain area, who are prepared to participate in a course of technical proficiency capacitation, and whose "thematic universe" we already know, what do we do, and how do we act? The "treatment" of the theme researched considers the "reduction" and the "codification"[9] of the themes which make up

9. See *Pedagogy...*

the program as a structure, that is, as a system of relationships in which one theme leads obligatorily to others, all joined in units and sub-units within the program.

Thematic "codifications" are the representations of existential situations—situations of work in the fields where the peasants are using some less efficient method of working; situations representing scenes apparently dissociated from technical process and yet which have some relation to them, etc. The interlocutor-Subjects, faced with a pedagogical "codification"[10] (problem-situation), which as I said represents a given existential situation, concentrate on it, seeking through dialogue the significant comprehension of its meaning. Since this is a gnosiological condition in which the knowable object is the existential situation represented in it, it is not the role of educators to narrate to the educatees (the peasants) what in their opinion constitutes their knowledge of reality or of the technical dimension involved in it. On the contrary, their task is to challenge the peasants once again to penetrate the significance of the thematic content with which they are confronted.

The codification represents an existential situation, a situation "lived" by the peasants, which they either do not "enter into" in the process of living it, or if they do, their "entering into" is merely being aware of the situation. The de-coding, as an act of knowing, allows them to "enter into" their own prior perceptions of their reality. De-coding is thus a dialectical moment in time, in which the consciousness,

---

10. The pedagogical codification can be distinguished from the advertising slogan because:

A. The nucleus of the former consists of a broad significatum expressed by a number of information factors; the nucleus of the latter consists of a singular, concise significatum, made up of "announcing factors" pointing in a single direction imposed by the propagandist;

B. The former, which is problem-posing, implies a de-coding to be carried out in dialogue between the educator-educatee and the educatee-educator.

Precisely because the latter has a single "announcing" nucleus, it only needs a single de-coding. Faced with an advertising slogan, two million inhabitants of Santiago de-code it in the same way; otherwise it would be publicity gone wrong.

C. In the former there is true communication, which is intercommunication.

The latter shows "communiqués." The former "critiques," the latter "simplifies" (through *naïveté,* one of the levels of perception of reality).

concentrated on the challenge of the codification, rebuilds its power of reflection in the "entering into" of present understanding which progresses towards a new understanding. Through this process, the peasants progressively recognize that it is they who transform the world. If cutting down a tree, chopping it into sections, making planks of it and using them to make tables and chairs previously meant little more than just physical work, these acts with the aid of "re-entering into," now take on the true significance they should have: that of praxis. Table and chairs will never again be just table and chairs. They are something more. They are the products of a person's work. S/he would have to begin by this discovery if s/he were to learn to make them better.

The first moment in the de-coding process seems to be that in which the educatees begin to describe the elements of the codification, which make up the whole for them. But in fact there is a moment in time which precedes this. It is the moment when the consciousness directed towards the codification apprehends it as a whole. In general it is in a person's silence that this occurs. "Entering into" takes place in the moment when the consciousness establishes relations with the object of its intentionality. The descriptive stage is a second moment in the process, when the totality undergoing the "entering into" process is split. This splitting does not end the action of apprehending the codification as a whole. It is a movement in which the Subject as it were glimpses reality from within. In a third moment in time, the Subject in conjunction with others returns to the previous state of "entering into" in which to take in the coded situation as a whole. The Subject prepares itself in this way to see the situation as a structure in which the various elements are found in a closely knit relationship. As the critical perception is heightened, and as it becomes impossible to accept "focalist" explanations of reality, the fourth moment[11] in the de-coding process takes place. In this fourth moment, the Subject achieves the critical analysis of what is repre-

---

11. See José Luis Fiori: "Dialectics and Liberty: Two Dimensions of the Search for a Theme," *op. cit.*

sented by the codification, and as its content expresses his or her own reality, the criticism is of this.

All the steps mentioned here, which are not so rigidly separated as their description implies, form part of the conscientization process, which results in men and women being able to achieve their critical insertion in reality. Education which does not attempt to make this effort, which rather insists on the transmission of *communiqués*, on the extension of technical contents, cannot conceal its dehumanizing aspect. The agronomist-educators whose work requires that the peasants receive technical proficiency capacitation—I have said it already but it would be good to repeat it—cannot ignore it as a process of real knowing. They cannot use technical proficiency capacitation for its own sake, nor purely and exclusively as a means of increasing production, which without a doubt, is indispensable. As well as being a means of increasing production, which is a social phenomenon, technical proficiency capacitation should, as a process, become an object of reflection for the peasants. This reflection should help them discover the whole complex of relationships in which this capacitation is involved.

To take a more critical and a more historical viewpoint, this is precisely why not only technical proficiency capacitation but any other popular dimension of education in agrarian reform or otherwise, in Latin America and the Third World in general, must be associated with the effort being made so that simple human beings, as beings prevented from existing as people, can distinguish themselves as human beings. Chilean educators endeavoring to put into practice this conception of education in their work with the peasants have frequently quoted in their reports comments made by the peasants, such as: "There is no difference between humans and animals; when there is, the latter have the advantage—they are freer than we are. . . ." I have frequently mentioned the coding of themes, introducing the reader to a previous study of mine which has been quoted on various occasions.[12] This codification represents an existential situa-

---

12. See *Pedagogy of the Oppressed*, op. cit.

tion whose content leads to the central theme to be analyzed. It can be represented by a photograph, a drawing, or equally well by a poster. The object representing the codification— be it photograph, drawing or poster—is merely, however, a point of reference. A visual point of reference is just that and no more. It can just as well be used as an efficient expedient for "domestication" as for purposes of liberation.

My preoccupation throughout this essay has been to illuminate the principles and the basic aspects of an education which will be "the practice of freedom." What is important is that the agronomist-educator should know, whatever points of reference s/he may have at his or her disposal, that these are secondary, and are only justifiable if they are used in an undertaking which aims at liberation. This undertaking requires something basic from any one of the Subjects participating in it—that they ask themselves if they really believe in the people, in ordinary people, in the peasants. If they are really capable of communing with them, of "proclaiming" the world with them. If they are incapable of believing in the peasants, of communing with them, they will at best be cold technicians. They will probably be technocrats, or even good reformers. But they will never be educators who will carry out radical transformations.